STRENGTH-CENTERED COUNSELING

*This book is dedicated those mentors, students, and colleagues who have nourished
our growth both professionally and personally. The spirit of their influence laces every word of the book in their
recognition of the value of hope, the importance of possibilities, and the nature of change from a perspective of strength.*

*This book honors the effort of counselors who daily engage in the noble purpose of making a
difference in the lives of others, and by doing so, make a difference in themselves.*

Colin Ward and Teri Reuter

*This book is dedicated to my wife, Laurie, whose loving support and encouragement has
made this project possible, and to the memory of my mentor and friend, Reese House.*

–CW

For Guido, Nick, and George

–TR

STRENGTH-CENTERED COUNSELING

INTEGRATING POSTMODERN APPROACHES AND SKILLS WITH PRACTICE

COLIN C. WARD

CENTRAL MICHIGAN UNIVERSITY

TERI REUTER

Los Angeles | London | New Delhi
Singapore | Washington DC

For information:

SAGE Publications, Inc.
2455 Teller Road
Thousand Oaks, California 91320
E-mail: order@sagepub.com

SAGE Publications Ltd.
1 Oliver's Yard
55 City Road
London EC1Y 1SP
United Kingdom

SAGE Publications India Pvt. Ltd.
B 1/I 1 Mohan Cooperative Industrial Area
Mathura Road, New Delhi 110 044
India

SAGE Publications Asia-Pacific Pte. Ltd.
33 Pekin Street #02-01
Far East Square
Singapore 048763

Printed in the United States of America.

Library of Congress Cataloging-in-Publication Data

Ward, Colin C.
Strength-centered counseling : integrating postmodern approaches and skills with practice/ Colin C. Ward, Teri Reuter.
    p. cm.
Includes bibliographical references and index.
ISBN 978-1-4129-7329-8 (pbk.)
    1. Humanistic counseling. 2. Client-centered psychotherapy. 3. Counseling. I. Reuter, Teri. II. Title.

BF636.7.H86W37 2011
158'.3—dc22   2010015051

This book is printed on acid-free paper.

10   11   12   13   14   10   9   8   7   6   5   4   3   2   1

Acquisitions Editor:	Kassie Graves
Editorial Assistant:	Veronica Novak
Production Editor:	Karen Wiley
Copy Editor:	Kristin Bergstad
Typesetter:	C&M Digitals (P) Ltd.
Proofreader:	Caryne Brown
Indexer:	Rick Hurd
Cover Designer:	Janet Kiesel
Marketing Manager:	Stephanie Adams

Contents

List of Figures and Tables

List of Figures

List of Tables

Preface

*S*trength-Centered Counseling: Integrating Postmodern Approaches and Skills With Practice began as a response to students asking Colin Ward for something more tangible to take with them after completing one of his seminars. He guided us through a process of changing our perspectives and invited us to question just about everything we had learned about being and becoming counselors. His seminars were transforming. He would often say, "You cannot not know something once you know it," and although we were curious and ready for something new as we entered his classroom, few of us understood the transformative power of the "knowing" about strength-centered counseling. It shifted the perception we had of ourselves as well as our interactions. Although this book was intended as a guide for counselors in their professional work, I have come to believe it may be even more for counselors in their personal lives. It is both—and this is consistent with the postmodern principles on which strength-centered counseling is founded.

Following my training with Colin and feeling compelled to process all of my other class information through a strength-centered perspective, I approached him about doing an independent study. From that meeting emerged an idea for a straightforward book designed for counselors wishing to synthesize the principles and skills of strength-centered counseling into their professional practices. From class and research notes, training presentations, and the various interview guides developed over the years, the book began. We incorporated the feedback and training experiences of counselors whose voices offer insight into the challenges and rewards of adopting this stance. Finally, I found that Colin's training materials and my own personal notes of the experience acted as a field guide in my development as a strength-centered counselor. They provided a reference point to remind me of "what I already knew" and to appreciate the value of working from an authentic life stance. It is my hope that this text does the same for you, reminding you of the transformative potential you can have with others, as well as with yourself.

Teri Reuter

Strength-Centered Counseling: Integrating Postmodern Approaches and Skills With Practice is a succinct description of the theoretical foundations and development of strength-centered counseling along with a practical explanation of working through three phases of counseling with clients. The strength-centered counseling model unifies postmodern schools of thought in order to guide practicing mental health providers who wish to incorporate strength-centered techniques and interventions with their existing clients as well as to offer graduate students in counselor education programs a foundation in an effective broad-application model of counseling.

We have divided *Strength-Centered Counseling: Integrating Postmodern Approaches and Skills With Practice* into three sections. Part I introduces the foundations of strength-centered counseling, distinguishing between modern and postmodern schools of thought and providing a synthesis of postmodern theories of therapeutic change under one overarching set of principles. Part II introduces and teaches the three phases of strength-centered counseling: Shared Understanding, Contracted Change, and Developed Lifestyle. In Part III, we address strength-centered counseling competence and offer a plan for developing and maintaining hope and wellness as a helping professional.

Although traditional approaches continue to dominate the landscape, an appreciation of postmodern models and a focus on client strengths is gaining acceptance. We see this trend continuing, especially when supported by an increased availability of appropriate core textbooks and supplemental supporting materials. We intend for our treatment of the phases of strength-centered counseling to leave you with clear direction and examples for integrating strength-centered counseling with existing clients and/or for use in counselor education programs. Especially as strength-centered counseling is not limited to practice with a specific client population, its principles and techniques can be used with clients of any age and across many themes.

ACKNOWLEDGMENTS

We would like to thank Kevin Gray of Kevin Gray Photographics, Grand Rapids, Michigan, for allowing us to include his artwork.

We gratefully acknowledge the following reviewers for their editorial insight: Joan Hartzke McIlroy, Lewis and Clark College; Jon Carlson, Govenors State University; Gonzalo Bacigalupe, University of Massachusetts, Boston; Elizabeth Vera, Loyola University Chicago; and Teresa McDowell, Lewis and Clark College. We would also like to thank the counselors whom we quote in the book for lending their voices to this project.

Foundations of Strength-Centered Counseling

The least of things with a meaning is worth more in life than the greatest of things without it.

–Carl Jung

The Essence of Strength-Centered Counseling

The eye sees only what the mind is prepared to comprehend.

–Henri Bergson

S *trength-Centered Counseling: Integrating Postmodern Approaches and Skills With Practice* provides a framework for the synthesis of postmodern theories of counseling. Our model can be incorporated effectively with the more traditional models of counseling, resolving the ambiguity about how postmodernism fits into everyday practice and results in more direct application of knowledge and skill sets for training in counselor education. We offer a practical and straightforward resource for a perspective and practice that elicits hope and provides clients opportunities to look at life from a context not only of problems and adversity but also of solutions, strengths, and possibilities. In addition, counselor educators and supervisors will find this book useful for guiding students and supervisees in learning the skills consistent with postmodern approaches under the unifying phases of Strength-Centered Counseling.

Traditionally, counseling theories have been considered accurate reflections of the human experience, contending that the problems individuals face result from deficits within themselves or their environments. Whether cognitive, behavioral, systemic, or psychodynamic in nature, modernist theories have been the primary influence on the training and education of counselors. Contrasting with these traditional, linear models of counseling, postmodern approaches to therapeutic change have developed over the past few decades. These theories highlight and utilize individual strengths, focus on developing solutions in concert with the individual and family, and view change as a dynamic and fluid process. Specifically, Solution-Focused Counseling, Narrative Therapy, and Motivational Interviewing share common principles for understanding and addressing interpersonal struggles; nevertheless, they have developed independently from one another, and for that reason, are not viewed as a single organized model of change. With the growing evolution of positive psychology and influence of wellness counseling as well as the demonstrated impact of hope and resiliency in overcoming life's challenges, an integrated postmodern counseling framework is needed for both counselors and counselor educators.

Strength-centered counseling is a set of perspectives and a practice that promotes change by recognizing the strengths inherent in every human struggle and reflected in adverse challenges.

This is also a book that encourages counselors to embrace the empowerment of hope not just with their clientele, but with themselves as well. If mental health practitioners have faith in the unique and surprising resources of people as they struggle for a better life, they will find such. If they do not, they will not, and over time, can be left with only a growing cynicism about the human experience of change, growth, and transformation. A strength-centered perspective assists counselors in remaining open to personal qualities that assist others and themselves with keeping illness at bay: a perspective that acknowledges that people are more than the sum of their symptoms and far more than the limitations placed on them by the experts sought out for help.

Richard Selzer (1976) reflected on the differing perspectives of the doctor–patient relationship in his book, *Mortal Lessons: Notes on the Art of Surgery*. The following experience with a Tibetan healer illustrated Seltzer's misgivings regarding traditional medical diagnostic practices and highlighted the impact contrasting healing perspectives can have on client experiences.

Yeshi Dhonden steps to the bedside while the rest stand apart, watching. For a long time he gazes at the woman, favoring no part of her body with his eyes, but seeming to fix his glance at a place just above her supine form. I, too, study her. No physical sign or obvious symptom gives a clue to the nature of her disease.

At last he takes her hand, raising it in both of his own. Now he bends over the bed in a kind of crouching stance, his head drawn down into the collar of his robe. His eyes are closed as he feels for her pulse. In a moment he has found the spot, and for the next half hour he remains thus, suspended above the patient like some exotic golden bird with folded wings, holding the pulse of the woman beneath his fingers, cradling her hand in his. All the power of the man seems to have been drawn down into this one purpose. It is palpation of the pulse raised to the state of ritual. From the foot of the bed, where I stand, it is as though he and the patient have entered a special place of isolation, apartness, about which a vacancy hovers, and across which no violation is possible. After a moment the woman rests back upon her pillow. From time to time, she raises her head to look at the strange figure above her, and then sinks back once more. I cannot see their hands joined in a correspondence that is exclusive, intimate, his fingertips receiving the voice of her sick body through the rhythm and throb she offers at her wrist. All at once I am envious—not of him, not of Yeshi Dhonden for his gift of beauty and holiness, but of her. I want to be held like that, touched so, *received*. And I know that I, who have palpated a hundred thousand pulses, have not felt a single one. . . .

As he nears the door (to leave), the woman raises her head and calls out to him in a voice at once urgent and serene. "Thank you doctor," she says, and touches with her hand the place he had held on her wrist, as though to recapture something that had visited there. Yeshi Dhonden turns back for a moment to gaze at her, and then steps into the corridor. Rounds are at an end.

We are seated once more in the conference room. Yeshi Dhonden speaks now for the first time, in soft Tibetan sounds that I have never heard before. He has barely begun when the young interpreter begins to translate, the two voices continuing in tandem—a bilingual fugue, the one chasing the other. It is like the chanting of monks. He speaks of winds coursing through the body of the woman, currents that break against barriers, eddying. These vortices are in her blood, he says. The last spending of an imperfect heart. Between the chambers of her heart, long, long before she was born, a wind had come and blown open a deep gate that must never be opened. Through it charge the full waters of her river, as the mountain stream cascades in the springtime, battering, knocking loose the land, and flooding her breath. Thus he speaks, and is silent.

"May we now have the diagnosis?" a professor asks.

The host of these rounds, the man who knows answers. "Congenital heart disease," he says. "Interventricular septal defect, with resultant heart failure."

A gateway in the heart, I think. That must not be opened. Through in charge the full waters that flood her breath. So! Here then is the doctor listening to the sounds of the body to which the rest of us are deaf. (pp. 34–36)

Strength-centered counseling is not the absence of solid graduate training in clinical psychodiagnosis, but a style of being with others that is not distracted by it. The severity of the woman's condition was understood from two distinct perspectives. They are views of the same condition, unchanging and chronic, that provided differing experiences for the patient, and ultimately for the helper. In one, a diagnosis was likely "given" to the patient following a series of medical tests and exams; the other was an explanation that was "received" from the patient following a time together of being heard and understood. This then is the intent of strength-centered counseling: to assist individuals and families with understanding and embracing the pain of life from a perspective that recognizes the struggle, the unique and inherent personal qualities in confrontation of the struggle, and the potential of both the counselor and client to provide a relational context for eliciting hope, increasing a readiness for change, and mapping out action steps for change and life satisfaction.

Counseling practice toward this end embraces a set of nine core principles—the essence of strength-centered counseling. They illustrate change through a deliberate use of language to accentuate personal strengths inherent in every human struggle and reflected in each challenge of adversity. As Saleebey (2006) pointed out, a strength-based counseling is a style of helping in which, rather than focusing on problems, your eye turns toward possibilities. Possibilities may become lasting change through shared experience of understanding, respect, strength, resilience, dichotomy, language, wellness, hope, and authenticity.

PRINCIPLE 1: A SHARED UNDERSTANDING

People are understood by strengths, resources, and characteristics learned and brought to bear against life's evolving challenges and not by the weight of their histories. Counselors share with others the unique qualities and strengths demonstrated in their efforts to stand up to life's difficulties, promoting a hope for change. Strength-centered counseling demonstrates a sincere interest in the well-being of others and illustrates a *shared understanding* of who clients are and what they hope to become. Strength-centered counselors seek to understand not only how difficulties and problems impact people's lives but also how they reflect the hopes and preferences people have. A *shared understanding* encourages counselors to collaborate with their clients in establishing goals that sustain people with the courage, optimism, personal responsibility, interpersonal skills, perseverance, and purpose needed to overcome adversity. Rather than working as an expert labeler of individual deficits, it is far more helpful, and efficient, for counselors to build relationships with clients on a *shared understanding* of how clients experience their problem stories. Actively sharing the valor, loyalty, persistence, honesty, prudence, and acceptance inherent in confronting life's struggles allows clients to experience their stories and themselves differently, while building a personal knowledge necessary for change.

PRINCIPLE 2: SHARED RESPECT

Strength-centered counseling relies on respect for the influences of culture, gender, race, age, profession, financial and legal status, sexual orientation, religion, education, and the various roles people bring to their life perspective and personal understanding. By its very intent, strength-centered counseling is multicultural, and it is a collaborative discovery of those strengths, resources, perspectives, and activities in seeking "something different" in the lives of others. *Shared respect* is demonstrated when clients, rather than counselors, have the last word on what they need to improve their lives. The perception of reality is a unique experience that exists only in the eyes and mind of the beholder, and this requires counselors to accept and respect the worldview of clients, appreciate what they wish different, and remain curious about how language within and between sessions maintains despair as well as to how it can introduce hope, possibilities, and a readiness for change.

PRINCIPLE 3: SHARED STRENGTHS

Strength-centered counselors are competent in the skills necessary to elicit strengths often hidden by misery, protective strategies, and the failure to achieve goals set by others. It requires counselors to be trained in a language of strengths as well as in the skills necessary for cocreating action plans that offer the greatest hope to others for living optimal lives. The identification of strengths represents characteristics empathically understood by clients and counselors that confront threats to psychological wellness. They are central to effective goal setting because they ground a "preferred life" in familiar landmarks and contribute to the likelihood of successful therapeutic outcomes. Assisting clients and families with understanding their struggles through a context of strengths and possibilities, rather than personal deficits and problems, instills hope and the self-healing tendencies necessary for change. *Shared strengths* represent those qualities and characteristics reflected in every struggle to "right the ship" that often go unnoticed due to the urgency of life's storms.

PRINCIPLE 4: SHARED RESILIENCE

Strength-centered counseling seeks to build client resilience through a process of strength awareness and application. Counseling that recognizes and elicits personal strengths increases the resiliency patterns needed to manage stress, cope with adversity, and develop actions that increase clients' satisfaction with themselves and others long after counseling has ended. Individuals' recognition of their own resiliency efforts in the face of life's struggles provides a route to authentic self-esteem. Understanding how individuals and families have been "stretched" by life's struggles provides a window into those strength characteristics that both support and distract in their fight for personal freedom. The intent of the counseling relationship, therefore, is to restore clients' belief in themselves and the control they have over events in their lives, leading to a *shared resilience* for the present and the future.

PRINCIPLE 5: SHARED DICHOTOMIES

Strength-centered counselors believe that people have the capacity to explore multiple sides of an experience. Where there are deficits, there are strengths; where problems arise, there are preferences; where there is resistance, there is also anticipation; where there is illness, there are opportunities for wellness; and where despair resides, hope lives also. Clients and families are influencing their lives all the time, even in the most dismal circumstances. It is not only that a client is depressed, but also how the client has been able to keep depression at bay. It is not only that a client is worried, but also how the client has been able to keep worry from taking over. Depression and worry are simply by-products in the pursuit of a better life, the hope for something more and different, and the efforts reflected in every struggle. A *shared dichotomy* is also insight into how the very strengths we so often engage to solve life's struggles may be precisely what stand in the way. Assisting others with understanding personal strength dichotomies can better support individuals and families by broadening their array of available strengths in order to address life's struggles.

PRINCIPLE 6: SHARED LANGUAGE

Strength-centered counselors depend on the strategic use of language to elicit meaning and cocreate possibilities with individuals and families. The dialogue between the client and counselor is deliberately shifted from a "problem saturated" worldview to one of hope, choice, and renewal. This *shared language* is at the heart of every technique and requires counselors to interact differently as well as think differently about clients. As the primary tool in therapy, language can elicit meanings that naturally occur in making sense of life challenges so as to assist others with perceiving themselves in ways that make standing up to these challenges possible. Within a trusting and empathic relationship, a strength-centered counselor seeks to shift how people describe themselves in relationship to the problems they wish resolved. It is not the removal of an irrational thought, an inappropriate behavior, or even how best to live with a personal deficit, but the addition of something else: possibilities, solutions, hope, and strengths.

PRINCIPLE 7: SHARED WELLNESS

Strength-centered counseling embodies a belief in personal wellness. Therapies that focus solely on problem resolution often fail to directly address lifestyle patterns that represent health beyond the absence of the initial concerns. The strengths needed to stand up to adversity are the same strengths needed to increase optimal health and well-being. By understanding human struggles through a perspective of strengths, counselors are able to identify those resilient life patterns and skills needed to address clients' initial concerns as well as lifestyle choices for increasing personal wellness. In addition, strength-centered counselors practice *shared wellness* so as to better withstand the professional struggles and fatigue that can accompany a career devoted to helping others.

PRINCIPLE 8: SHARED HOPE

Strength-centered counselors approach each encounter from a perspective of unwavering *shared hope*. Having faith in the unique and surprising resources of people as they confront insurmountable odds against a better life provides the greatest likelihood for recognizing the strengths in others and the often imperceptible movements of change. This is the cornerstone of personal resilience necessary for life satisfaction and fulfilled relationships. Assisting clients and families with understanding their struggles through a context of strengths and possibilities, rather than personal deficits and problems, instills a hope for change. It is therefore necessary that strength-centered counselors be competent in the skills and strategies for instilling hope in others.

PRINCIPLE 9: SHARED AUTHENTICITY

Learning the skills associated with strength-centered counseling is largely dependent on the willingness and ability of counselors to apply a strength-centered perspective in their personal lives. This involves developing equitable relationships, self-respect, and an appreciation that life choices different from one's own are equally valid. Personal and professional *shared authenticity* acknowledges the connection between a strength-centered counselor's choice of language and its influence on reality—discussing opportunities rather than limitations and challenges rather than setbacks. *Shared authenticity* also embodies a professional commitment to clients through a personal commitment to wellness and self-care.

These nine core principles (see Table 1.1) are the foundation of strength-centered counseling and support the interactions between clients and counselors, moving individuals and families from the possibility of overcoming adversity to realizing a preferred life. Counseling students and counselor educators should come to appreciate the integrated nature of these core principles as the essence of adopting a strength-centered perspective for work with clients, collaboration with colleagues, and their personal interactions.

Table 1.1	Essential Principles of Strength-Centered Counseling

Essential Principles of Strength-Centered Counseling	*Description*
1. Shared Understanding	Strength-centered counselors share with others the unique qualities and strengths demonstrated in their efforts to stand up to life's difficulties, promoting hope for change.
2. Shared Respect	Strength-centered counseling relies on respect for the influences of culture, gender, race, age, profession, financial and legal status, sexual orientation, religion, education, and the various roles people bring to their life perspective and personal understanding.
3. Shared Strengths	Strength-centered counselors are trained in the recognition and language of strengths as well as the skills necessary for cocreating action plans that are strength centered and offer the greatest hope to others for living optimal lives.
4. Shared Resilience	Strength-centered counseling that recognizes and elicits personal strengths increases the resiliency needed to manage stress, cope with adversity, and develop actions that increase clients' satisfaction with themselves and others long after counseling has ended.
5. Shared Dichotomies	Strength-centered counselors assist individuals and families with understanding personal strengths in order to broaden the array of their available strengths for better addressing life's struggles.
6. Shared Language	Strength-centered counselors use language as the primary tool in therapy to elicit meanings that naturally occur in making sense of life challenges so as to assist others with perceiving themselves in ways that make these challenges surmountable.
7. Shared Wellness	Strength-centered counselors are able to identify those resilient qualities and skills needed to address clients' initial concerns as well as lifestyle choices for increasing personal wellness by understanding human struggles through a perspective of strengths.
8. Shared Hope	Strength-centered counselors believe that having faith in the unique and surprising resources of people as they confront insurmountable odds to a better life provides the greatest likelihood for recognizing the strengths in others and the often imperceptible movements of change.
9. Shared Authenticity	The willingness and ability of strength-centered counselors to apply a strength-centered perspective in both their professional and personal lives allows them to experience shared authenticity with their clients and colleagues.

Strength-Centered Counseling: Integrating Postmodern Approaches and Skills With Practice is presented in three sections. In Part I we continue with the fundamentals, describing how strength-centered counseling works as a synthesis of postmodern models of counseling, explaining the integral role language plays in moving people toward lasting change. In Part II we introduce the three phases of strength-centered counseling: Shared Understanding, Contracted Change, and Developed Lifestyle. Along with the descriptions of each phase, we will guide you in incorporating strength-centered counseling techniques and interventions with existing clients. In Part III we link the principles and application of strength-centered counseling to professional practice and personal life, including a Professional Plan for Hope and Wellness that outlines steps for continued growth as a strength-centered counselor.

We have presented the phases of strength-centered counseling as a linear model; however, we hope to convey the nonlinear nature of moving *among* the phases as you work with clients and colleagues. While the presentation of the phases suggests that the steps happen in chronological order, experience will show you that no particular order is necessary or even more effective than another. Competent strength-centered counselors experience an internal integration of the theoretical principles and the techniques while interventions emerge naturally during interactions with clients and colleagues.

The shift required in your theoretical perspective as well as the language necessary for working through the phases of strength-centered counseling can be difficult. To provide a "normalcy" to this learning discomfort, we have included quotes from counselors who have worked with us in strength-centered training, classes, and seminars. Hearing their voices may allow you to connect with the material in a more personal way.

The chapters also include learning and professional growth activities for anchoring strength-centered concepts and skills. Engaging in these activities with a learning partner is very effective; however, in the case that a learning partner is not available, working individually with the aid of a journal can also be both effective and personally rewarding. Throughout the chapters you will notice sun-shaped icons indicating that additional details and guidance for processing activities and descriptions are available on our Web site through SAGE Publications: www.sagepub.com/wardreuter or on the DVD that accompanies the book.

Emergence of Postmodernism

A work can become modern only if it is first postmodern. Postmodernism thus under-stood is not modernism at its end but in the nascent state, and this state is constant.

–François, de La Rochefoucauld

Understanding the difference between modernism and postmodernism is to understand differing perceptions of change. Whereas one is predictable and consistent, the other is consistently unpredictable and evolving. Appreciating the unique clinical intent that modernism and postmodernism each contribute to the counseling relationship can assist counselors with better understanding their work with others while providing a foundation for understanding postmodern influences on strength-centered counseling. Because these terms are often misunderstood by students of counseling as well as practicing mental health professionals, the following is an attempt to briefly explore the differences between these two perspectives.

MODERN APPROACHES

Traditionally, counseling theories have been considered accurate reflections of the human experience, contending that the problems individuals face result from deficits within themselves or their environments. Whether cognitive, behavioral, or psychodynamic in nature, modernist theories consider truth as fundamentally singular and objectively veri-fiable (D'Andrea, 2000). Counselors become *objective observers* of the unconscious (psy-chodynamic), mental structures (cognitive), and environmental contingencies (behavioral) representing clients' personal deficits. These theories break people down into diagnostic categories, so that problems associated with their pathologies can be addressed. This is the overriding intent of modernist approaches to human change: to identify and organize infor-mation into a diagnostic schema that may lead to more effective methods of helping clients (Seligman, 1996).

Modern counseling approaches also view the human experience in terms of a two-dimensional perspective. Wellness is perceived as the absence of disease and/or the remission of a disorder; behavior is assessed as appropriate/functional or inappropriate/dysfunctional; and cognitions are represented by those that are rational in contrast with those that are irrational and self-defeating. Furthermore, the interpretative skills of the counselor and her or his command of a "pathology" language as referenced in the *Diagnostic and Statistical Manual (DSM)* "provide clear descriptions of diagnostic categories in order to enable clinicians and investigators to diagnose, communicate about, study, and treat people with the various mental disorders" (American Psychiatric Association, 1994, p. xxvii). The inherent simplicity of a two-dimensional view creates a straightforward diagnostic system that can apply to any given individual where (a) normal and abnormal are a measurable reality, (b) people receiving counseling must have a clinical disorder, and (c) the counselor is an unbiased perceiver of these realities and an accurate judge of disorders (Fong, 1993). Discovering the cause of an illness where symptoms are assessed and translated into prescribed treatment protocols is the heart of a modernist approach to therapeutic change. This *illness ideology* portrays people as victims of intrapsychic and biological forces beyond their control, and as such, in need of benevolent helpers to manage their symptoms (Maddux, 2002). From this perspective, patients are in need of experts to guide and instruct them in reducing the progression of their disabling emotional, cognitive, and/or behavioral symptoms.

POSTMODERN APPROACHES

Contrasting with these traditional, linear models of counseling, postmodern approaches to therapeutic change do not posit one, real truth about the human experience. These theories, developed over the past few decades, emphasize a constructed nature of knowledge where the world, and our experience of it, exists in the eyes and mind unique to each beholder. Combs's (1954) early theory on perception explained that "how a person behaves will be a direct outgrowth of the perceptions existing at any moment" (p. 65). These perceptions are constantly in a state of revision influenced by interaction with others, culture, and society at large. In other words, it is not so much an understanding of "multiple realities" as it is that perceptions of ourselves and the world around us are unique, varied, and "real" for the perceiver. Heider (1958), in explaining the tenets of attribution theory, concurred with this idea and concluded that people act according to their beliefs, whether or not counselors perceive those beliefs to be accurate, valid, or *based on reality*.

The intent of a postmodern approach is not to impose a single truth or to quantify the experience of another, but to approach each counseling encounter sensitive to the perspective that others bring to the change process (Hansen, 2007). In much the same way you are interpreting the text on this page, the text is transformed and constructed by your idiosyncratic processing (Flax, 1990; Spence, 1982). Perception is essentially a function of meaning, and as such will shift according to how people make sense of themselves and others—especially when challenged by adversity and the emotional/cognitive dissonance that can ensue (Hansen, 2007). The illusion in Figure 2.1 is an example of how our minds attempt to find meaning from ambiguous stimuli. As you look at the cube, are the lines crooked or straight? Do the adjacent lines appear to slide past each other? With a ruler or straightedge, check your perceptions.

Figure 2.1	The Café Wall Illusion

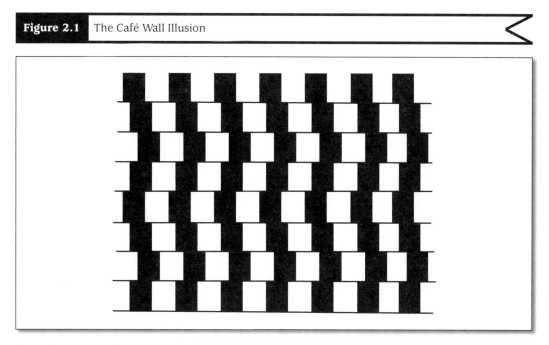

Source: Gregory & Heard (1979).

The Café Wall Illusion (Gregory & Heard, 1979) represents the perceptual struggle when attempting to assign meaning to a three-dimensional image from a two-dimensional perspective. Although our visual system is capable of performing complex processing of information received from the eyes in order to extract meaningful perceptions, some visual stimuli cannot be perceived in a way that can be measured. Traditional counseling models view human change from a two-dimensional perspective. People are free of disease or they are not. Behavior is interpreted as functional or dysfunctional, and client thoughts are either rational or irrational. Postmodernism contends that human experiences (and one's perception of them) are far too complex to be described in two-dimensional terms (see Table 2.1). It is an acceptance of the unique, meaningful experiences of others and the inherent wisdom and strengths they bring to the change process. From a postmodern perspective, counseling encounters become a "meaning-generating system" (De Shazer, 1991, p. 64), where client perspectives are broadened and revised to include a wider range of options for self-determined change.

It is common during periods of intense stress to see only that which is most urgent, and usually from such a close perspective that life looks and feels overwhelming. If the only view of the Grand Canyon you had was from the bottom, you would have little appreciation for the length, breadth, and unique features it embodies. The intent of postmodern counseling is to assist others with viewing and describing their world from multiple and broader points of view. This becomes an appreciation of the canyon, the hiker, and the relationship between the canyon and hiker. The postmodern counselor, therefore, seeks not to interpret clients' perspectives, but to provide opportunities for eliciting expanded and alternate meanings of their experiences and of themselves.

Table 2.1   Postmodernism and Modernism

Postmodernism	Modernism
Truth as Perception	*Truth as Singular and Objective*
– Reality is unique and exists only in the eyes and mind of the beholder. – Perceptions are influenced by others, culture, and society.	– Reality is measurable and verifiable. – Personality theories offer accurate reflections on the human experience.
Multidimensional View of Experience	*Two-Dimensional View of Experience*
– Behavior is a direct outgrowth of perceptions (beliefs) at any given moment. – Perception is a function of meaning and will be unique for individuals as they construct their understanding of themselves and others through language. – People will act according to their perceptions (beliefs) whether or not counselors agree or disagree.	– Counselors understand wellness across two dimensions: disease or health. – Counselors understand behavior across two dimensions: inappropriate or appropriate. – Counselors understand cognitions across two dimensions: irrational or rational.
Treatment Founded on Personal Resilience	*Treatment Founded on Pathology*
– Life can be problematic, and people have unique and inherent qualities in standing up to adversity. – Counseling that recognizes and elicits personal strengths increases the resiliency needed to manage stress, cope with adversity, and develop actions that increase clients' satisfaction with themselves and others long after counseling has ended.	– Problems result from individual deficits. – Individual deficits are reduced to diagnostic categories. – Diagnostic categories lead to prescribed treatments.
Counselor as a Curious Conversationalist	*Counselor as Assessor and Observer*
– Counselors appreciate that clients are experts on their own lives. – Language is a key intervention for eliciting understanding and shifting perceptions. – Counselors see the perception of problems as separate (unique) from the people perceiving them. – Human change is a reflective process in which clients are active participants.	– Counselors have competent command of pathology language. – Counselors are expert observers of the unconscious (psychodynamic), mental structures (cognitive), and client environment (behavioral). – Counselors discover an illness cause and prescribe treatment in which clients are passive recipients of an expert's "care and cure."

Strength-centered counseling is grounded on the postmodern premise that personal realities are in constant flux, being revised and adapted to the world around them. It is the idea that people do not belong to the world; they exist in a world of possibilities that become realities through their conscious interpretation (Santamaria, 1990). It becomes less about the story itself, and more about how the story defines the storyteller: an attunement to what is being experienced of what is being said. This requires counselors to accept the worldview of clients, appreciate what they wish to be different, and remain curious about how language maintains despair as well as how it can introduce hope, possibilities, and a readiness for change. Therapeutic change occurs through *experiencing* a constructed truth within the client–counselor interaction, rather than an absolute truth *discovered* solely by the counselor, and the constructed truth between the client and counselor is largely an experience of *language*. It is through language that people make sense of their lives and themselves. In conversation and interaction with others, life stories are ascribed meanings that are used to define one's sense of self, shape behavior, and orient oneself in the world (Dimaggio, Salvatore, Azzara, & Catania, 2003; Hansen, 2007; Hoffman, Stewart, Warren, & Meek, 2009; Maturana & Varela, 1987).

> For me, the most interesting part of the strength-centered perspective is that it is based on the postmodernist philosophy that everything exists at once: frustration and hope; inaction and action; the problem and the strength to overcome it. It is a different way of thinking than what I am used to, but it makes complete sense. The idea that the strength and skills to reach our goals already exist within us is incredibly motivating! What's more, the process of externalizing the problem while owning or internalizing our strengths just feels more positive and refreshing than dwelling on or analyzing our deepest, darkest wounds. I don't believe these "wounds" (or the problem) should just be brushed under the rug, though. Identifying them and referring to them seems necessary. Still, the problem should not be the primary focus. –Jennifer C.

Strength-centered counseling is a postmodern perspective of the helping relationships between counselors and clients and acts as a unifying umbrella for other postmodern approaches, including solution-focused counseling (SFC), narrative counseling (NC), and motivational interviewing (MI). These approaches share common principles, and although they have developed relatively independently from one another, they provide a foundation for taking the next step toward understanding the intent and clinical application of strength-centered counseling. Chapter 3 offers an overview of these foundational principles along with an explanation of how they are supportive of strength-centered counseling.

Postmodern Counseling

Self-realization can be encouraged if the therapist has a profound knowledge, not of therapeutic theories and formulations, but of people and their personal experiences.

–Jurgen Ruesch

The most common counseling approaches founded on postmodern principles are Solution Focused Counseling (SFC), Narrative Counseling (NC), and Motivational Interviewing (MI). Although each is unique in how it instructs counselors to interact and apply postmodern principles of change, each shares common themes in its overall approach. First, SFC, NC, and MI articulate a sincere respect for clients and the difficulties that have led them to seek counseling. Clients are viewed as the experts on their lives. The counselor promotes a relationship that is, as much as possible, nonjudgmental and accepting of the experiences, worldviews, and the inherent resilient qualities individuals and families present in their struggle against life's challenges. As Lambert (1992) pointed out in his review of counseling outcomes, the counseling relationship can empower and motivate people in the process of change. As an empathic participant in the counseling process, the counselor becomes a "curious conversationalist" (G. Miller, 2001, p. 80), described as being in a "not-knowing" position by Anderson and Goolishian (1992). They wrote that the

> not-knowing position entails a general attitude or stance in which the therapist's actions communicate an abundant, genuine curiosity. That is, the therapist's actions and attitudes express a need to know more about what has been said, rather than convey preconceived opinions and expectations about the client, the problem, or what must be changed. The therapist, therefore, positions himself or herself in such a way as always to be in a state of "being informed" by the client. (p. 29)

Second, in each approach, language is strategically utilized to elicit meaning. Because reality is the product of language, the counselor actively *cocreates* possibilities with individuals and families. Emergent from the counseling interaction are solutions, strengths, and self-perceptions that enhance clients' willingness to promote change in their lives. Shifting from a "problem-saturated" worldview to one of hope and possibilities requires counselors to consider the language they apply not just to others but also to themselves. In essence, the use of language in postmodern approaches of counseling becomes a reflective process for both counselors and clients.

Because the constructed truth between the client and counselor is largely an experience of language, the strategic use of language to elicit new meanings, expand perspectives, and encourage change is central to a postmodern approach to counseling. This language assists helping professionals shift from seeing only risk to seeing resilience and strength while highlighting people's choices. It also creates an assumption of accountability, rather than blame or determinism. As Bertolino and O'Hanlon (2002) articulated, "If the person is not the problem, but has a certain relationship to the problem, then the relationship can change . . . if the problem is trying to recruit a client, he or she can refuse to join" (p. 133). This is not to be confused with merely *wishing* away problems or creating new *fictions*. As the primary tool in therapy, language elicits meanings, making sense of life challenges and creating the possibilities that allow clients to stand up to present and future adversity.

The final commonality among the three postmodern counseling approaches is that of reflective learning. It is described as the process whereby people meaningfully reconstruct experiences utilizing a repertoire of understandings, images, and actions to reconstruct a troubling situation so that problem-solving interventions can be generated (Ward & House, 1998). This is reminiscent of Bowen's (1978) idea of differentiation where personal growth is contingent on a self-reflective process to modulate emotionality in the face of tension or conflict; or Mezirow's (1994) contention that personal meaning is created when individuals are faced with unfamiliar situations and divergent experiences. In contrast to modernist or traditional approaches of counseling, which can seek to reduce client discomfort, SFC, NC, and MI seek to embrace such discomfort as well as the ambivalence regarding personal inconsistencies. Within a trusting and empathic relationship, a postmodern counselor seeks to shift how people describe themselves in relationship to the problems they wish resolved. It is not the removal of an irrational thought, an inappropriate behavior, or even how best to live with a personal deficit, but the addition of something else: possibilities, solutions, hope, and strengths.

Strength-centered counseling shares in the commonalities among solution-focused counseling, narrative counseling, and motivational interviewing; an empathic and accepting counseling relationship, the strategic use of language for eliciting alternate life interpretations, and understanding clinical change as a reflective process of personal learning (see Table 3.1). Although unique in its emphasis on strengths for the development of personal resilience, strength-centered counseling also incorporates many of the tools consistent with the commonalities above as well those unique to each of these postmodern approaches—SFC, NC, and MI. Table 3.1 offers a brief explanation of the intent and examples of how each addresses changes with clients and families.

Table 3.1	Common Principles of Postmodern Counseling

Nonjudgment and Acceptance
- Respect for client as the experts from a "not-knowing" position
- Empathic curiosity about client/family worldview

Meaning Eliciting Language
- Cocreate possibilities
- Perceptual shift from seeing only risk to seeing resilience and strength

Reflective Learning
- Opportunities to reconstruct experiences in generating problem solving
- Modulating emotions in the face of tension and conflict for personal growth

SOLUTION-FOCUSED COUNSELING

Solution-focused practice is a short-term approach where counselors attend to solutions or exceptions to the problem more than to problems themselves (De Jong & Berg, 2002). It is grounded in family systems, cognitive, and communication theories that seek to move clients away from problem talk to talk focused on solutions. Three central ideas guide SFC: speaking about and visualizing change increases the likelihood of change, there are exceptions to the most problematic patterns, and even the smallest personal change can create ripple effects in various life areas. Solution-focused counselors invite clients and families to construct a conceptual model of their *futures* with concrete evidence of how their growth will be recognized (Cepeda & Davenport, 2006). Through the use of future goal-oriented questions, counselors attempt to cocreate with others a *language of possibilities* exemplified by O'Connell (1998), with the following change visualization questions for clients in sessions:

- What will you do to make sure you do not need to come back to see me?
- What do you think the possible obstacles might be and how will you overcome them?
- What do you need to remember if things get difficult for you again?
- With all the changes you are making, what will you tell me about yourself if I run into you at a supermarket six months from now?

This model also contends that people are victims of their own constructions of reality and inclined to view problems as always occurring, when, actually, problems tend to fade away at times. These "exceptions" to the problem often go unnoticed or are discounted as too small to be of any importance. Solution-focused counselors encourage an elaboration of exceptions in establishing client goals. Examples of questions eliciting exceptions include:

- When would you say you do not have the problem or you have the problem with less intensity?
- Can you think of any other time, either in the past or in recent weeks, you did not have the problem? How do you explain that this problem doesn't happen then?
- What is your guess about why you don't have this problem then? Where might you have gotten the idea to do it differently at those times?
- What is your guess about what others notice to be different about you when you have a better handle on your problems?

In contrast to more traditional counseling models, SFC utilizes therapeutic questions to elicit solution-oriented dialogues with clients and families. It represents an emphasis on a solution-building process where the experience of envisioning a preferred and client-directed future is far more important and empowering than those generated by others (e.g., counselors). It is this envisioning process that informs strength-centered counseling to emphasize not only preferred futures, but also on the preferred strengths clients and families will need to tap in order to see preferences become realities (see Table 3.2). The emphasis on language, and how it can both maintain despair as well as provide hope, is the foundational premise of Narrative Counseling.

Table 3.2	Current Postmodern Approaches	

Solution-Focused Counseling (De Shazer & Berg)

- Speaking about and visualizing change increases the likelihood of change.
- There are exceptions to even the most problematic patterns.
- Clients/families are invited to construct futures with concrete evidence as to how growth will be recognized.

Narrative Counseling (White & Epston)

- People are constantly telling stories (personal narrative) that describe who they are in the world to others and themselves.
- NC aids clients/families with constructing different narratives (perception) in relation to life events.
- Eliciting different past and future stories encourages "unique outcomes" to be developed.

Motivational Interviewing (W. R. Miller & Rollnick)

- MI is a client-centered, directive method for enhancing motivation to change by exploring and resolving the client's ambivalence.
- Clients/families are helped to resolve ambivalence in a direction that strengthens a desire for change (Stages of Change)

NARRATIVE COUNSELING

From an NC point of view, people are constantly telling stories that describe who they are as well as their position in the world to others and themselves (White & Epston, 1990). This method is grounded in the existential idea that individuals are unique in how they relate to the experiences of their lives (Boss, 1983) as well as to the internal perceptions they have of themselves. If these internal perceptions become *problem saturated,* self-denigrating beliefs and emotional suffering can result. The intent of NC is to assist individuals and families with eliciting new aspects of their stories so that "unique outcomes" can be constructed as well as future perceptions of themselves and others (White, 1989).

Furthermore, individuals often enter counseling enmeshing their sense of self with their problems. To assist people with appreciating themselves in separation from their problems, NC utilizes externalizing questions to elicit a self-identity apart from problem-saturated descriptions. The intent is to shift the focus onto the relationship between the person and the problem instead focusing on the problem-person. Examples of externalizing questions are below (Winslade & Monk, 2006):

- Can you think of a name to call this problem? What is it like (picture/metaphor)? Are there other problems that this one teams up with?
- How has the problem robbed you of what you want?
- How were you recruited into this way of thinking? What does the voice of (problem) whisper in your ear?
- What does the problem try to convince you of? If it had its way, how would you end up? What does the problem stand to gain? What does the problem stand to lose?
- How does the problem trick you in "getting the best of you"? What has the problem promised you?
- Would the problem (e.g., depression) want you in counseling? Did it try to keep you from coming? How much of your life does it control?
- What do you do to keep the problem at bay? Who else is an advocate in this with you? How have you been able to weaken the influence of the problem?

It is this externalizing process that highlights the unique contribution of NC to strength-centered counseling. Developing perceptual and emotional space between the person and the problem allows for the recognition of personal strengths and resilient qualities. Conversely, the recognition of personal strengths and resilient qualities can assist clients and families with defining themselves in separation from their life struggles (see Table 3.2). It is within this perceptual and emotional space that Motivational Interviewing attempts to intervene. MI emphasizes the process and experience of the difficulties associated with change and reaching personal life goals.

MOTIVATIONAL INTERVIEWING

That change is more than a yes or no decision, but a complex and dynamic process characterized by feelings of ambivalence and uncertainty is a fundamental belief of an MI approach. It is described as a client-centered, directive method for enhancing motivation to change by exploring and resolving the client's ambivalence (W. R. Miller & Rollnick, 2002). Developed as an alternative to traditional substance-use treatments, MI seeks to elicit the ambivalence and conflicting thoughts when important lifestyle changes are being considered. With MI, counselors assist clients in resolving this ambivalence in a direction that strengthens the client's desire to change (W. R. Miller & Rose, 2009). The counselor utilizes a strong empathic relationship, devoid of preconceived clinical goals, so that the advantages and disadvantages of the problem behavior as well as the advantages and disadvantages of changing are openly considered.

The intent of the approach is to highlight ambivalence while directly eliciting a conversation of change with clients and families. By exploring the benefits, dangers, and steps necessary when contemplating interpersonal decisions, a belief in the possibility of change increases. From an MI perspective, talking about the experience of change increases one's motivation for change (see Table 3.2) (Moyers & Martin, 2006; Moyers, Martin, Christopher, Houck, Tonigan, & Amrhein, 2007). Examples of how this might be elicited are as follows (W. R. Miller & Rollnick, 2002):

- What difficulties have you had in relation to your _____ (problem)?
- In what ways do you think this has impacted you or others?
- What worries you about your problem? What can you imagining happening to you?
- What do you think will happen if you do not make a change?
- What makes you think that you may need to make a change?
- What things make you think that you should not change?
- On a scale of one to five—one meaning not very motivated and 5 meaning very motivated—where would you rate your level of confidence today in doing something different?

Strength-centered counseling is rooted in the postmodern principles of solution-focused counseling, narrative counseling, and motivational interviewing and seeks to unite the approaches with an emphasis on increasing patterns of personal resilience. Through an awareness of strengths, life challenges are perceived as surmountable, where change becomes not only possible but inevitable.

PROFESSIONAL GROWTH ACTIVITY: HOPE AND ADVERSITY

With a learning partner, have a shared conversation around the following sequential focus questions:

Step 1: Talk about a time you felt hopeful about your life and circumstances. What was going on in your life that made you feel hopeful?

Step 2: Talk about what others might say are the qualities that keep you going in the face of stress and adversity.

Step 3: How have you reminded yourself to keep moving forward during these more difficult times?

Step 4: Share with each other your reaction to having this conversation.

Central Role of Language in Strength-Centered Counseling

C'est le point de vue qui crée l'objet. [It is the point of view that creates the object.]

–Ferdinand de Saussure

Traditional models of counseling often use a language based in clinical psychology working from a medical model to describe clients in terms of limitations and a focus on what clients cannot do (Smith, 2006). This language of pathology creates a perception of illness and undermines the role of responsibility in how clients navigate their own lives, looking at clients in counseling as victims of their diagnoses and denying them the reward of taking responsibility for coping behaviors that maintain their survival (Maddux, 2002). An alternative is language that highlights possibilities with a focus on what clients are already doing in order to cope, survive, and in some parts of their lives, even thrive. Using a strength-centered vocabulary aids counselors and clients in recognizing the often imperceptible movements toward change and a preferred life. Recognizing even the smallest success is evidence that a client possesses the strengths and resources necessary to withstand life's complex problems, and that such strengths might be put to use in other parts of the client's life. Without the deliberate use of this language, client strengths often go unrecognized, unnamed, and unused, sacrificing the chance for clients to realize that they already possess many of the strengths and resources necessary to meet life's challenges and increase their levels of resilience for facing future struggles. Just as new words are coined for new technologies, the following seeks to introduce a strength-centered vocabulary that reflects the vision of strength between a client and a counselor and between the client and himself or herself.

LANGUAGE AND MEANING

Meaning is the connection between communicators (i.e., client and counselor) and the language they use to construct reality. Language creates the reality that we perceive where two processes are happening at once. The first is that reality takes shape under the influence of language. The second is that language takes shape under the influence of reality (Beedham, 2005). Language influencing reality and reality influencing language are at work in the development and maintenance of the *illness ideology* within the field of counseling (Maddux, 2002). This language of clinical psychology has been used to describe interactions between therapists and individuals seeking help. The clinician completes formal intakes and assessments, assembles charts, identifies symptoms and selects diagnoses, and writes treatment plans with a focus on the removal or reduction of the patient's initial symptomology. It implies the care of a benevolent expert and utilizes terminology supporting an inequity between practitioners and recipients of care. In addition, this illness ideology continues to shape the counseling field through its influence on new counselors who subscribe to a model based on recognizing personal deficits rather than personal strengths, assets, and patterns of resilience.

Likewise the interrelationship between language and reality creates an alternative meaning when counseling professionals use a language of strengths for identifying positive human qualities that in daily life are often unacknowledged and unnamed. Use of strength-centered language can shift perception, for both the client and counselor, from seeing risks to also seeing resilience. Strength-centered language creates an equitable relationship between the client and counselor. As De Jong and Berg (1998) articulated, "Wittingly or unwittingly, the helping professions have encouraged practitioners to believe and act as though their perceptions about their clients' problems and solutions are more important to the helping process than are the clients' perceptions" (p. 19); therefore, a change in language and vocabulary plays more than just a supporting role in strength-centered counseling. The deliberate use of questions by counselors to elicit a shared language with clients about their strengths, hopes, and dreams as they confront personal fatigue, hopelessness, and overwhelming problems is the intent of strength-centered counseling and consistent with each phase of its application. Furthermore, a counseling context that recognizes and supports the development of strengths and resources within clients encourages equitable relationships between counselors and clients.

REALITY AND STRENGTH-CENTERED LANGUAGE

The reciprocal influence of language and reality during counseling sessions requires that strength-centered counselors understand and competently use a strength-centered vocabulary in order to demonstrate an authentic appreciation of a client's struggles. Frank (1987) asserted that therapeutic interaction is successful only to the extent that it helps clients transform the meanings of their experiences. Being able to elicit and recognize strengths in others requires counselors to have a vocabulary that can identify and elicit strengths from client and family experiences needed to transform general categories of strength (e.g., courage) to specific personal qualities (e.g., perseverance). This level of "concreteness" has long been described as crucial to communicating empathy (Patterson, 1974; Rogers, 1957) and allows clients an accurate understanding of how their strengths enhance, and possibly distract, in their efforts to overcome adversity. A clinical vocabulary that can concretely communicate strengths also provides a context in which to plan action steps for resolving life problems and increasing life satisfaction.

Strengths are not to be confused with merely *wishing away problems* or the creation of *new fictions*. They are not simply finding positive qualities from negative experiences (false reassurance) or providing clients with counselor-generated affirmations (a hoped-for truth). Rather, strengths are truths reflected in personal struggles and often in the presenting problems that clients seek to resolve. They highlight an unrecognized commitment of personal, physical, and spiritual survival and represent character virtues that confront threats to psychological well-being and act as buffers to mental illness (Peterson & Seligman, 2004). As the primary tool of strength-centered counselors, a strength vocabulary can elicit meanings that naturally occur in making sense of life challenges so as to assist others with perceiving themselves in ways that make standing up to adversity possible, even probable. Strength-centered language assists both counselor and client in shifting from a perspective of risk and fatigue, to one of resilience and interpersonal hope.

There is an old joke about a man who entered a clothing store to buy a new suit. Upon expressing his wish to the salesperson, he was presented with a suit for fitting. Although the man complained about one pant leg being too long, the salesperson instructed to the man to walk more on his toes. And although a jacket sleeve felt too short, the salesperson instructed the man to hunch up his shoulder. The next day the man was walking down the street in his new suit. While walking on his toes with one shoulder hunched up, he was noticed by two pedestrians. The first commented on how he walked and expressed how uncomfortable the man appeared. The other agreed, and added, "and doesn't he look good in that suit" (adapted from the *Dick Van Dyke Show*). Learning a strength-centered language can be much the same way: Although it has a beauty about it, it can feel quite uncomfortable at first. Finding the correct posture and tailoring the suit to fit one's measurements is the way to feel comfortable in this good-looking but ill-fitting suit. At first, new strength-centered counselors may appreciate the theoretical value of using strength-centered language but find the vocabulary unfamiliar and ill fitting; however, with exposure to and practice with the new vocabulary, a counselor is able to rely on the principles of strength-centered counseling and its use of language while discovering how to tailor the use of strength-centered language so that it is congruent with the counselor's personal communication style.

Finding a level of comfort with strength-centered language is similar to gaining fluency when learning a foreign language. A new speaker starts slowly, learning vocabulary words, moving to short phrases and dialogs, and after much practice begins to converse and demonstrate competence during interactions with native speakers. When learning any new language, trying it on for size presents personal and professional opportunities for getting more comfortable and confident with its application.

STRENGTH-CENTERED VOCABULARY COMPETENCE

Creating with the client a reality of possibilities and hope in the face of problems and adversity in part depends on a counselor's choice of words. A strength-centered counselor's communication competence develops as the counselor moves away from the language of traditional clinical psychology infused with *medicalized* terminology toward language focused on eliciting a unique understanding of an individual's struggle. Strength-centered language is infused with possibilities and is essential in creating an alternative reality for the client to realize the preferences, values, and strengths already present in managing his or her life circumstances.

Some individuals have little use for or little interest in learning a foreign language. Instead these speakers interact with others using only their own language. Even when traveling to other countries, the preference is to communicate in their mother tongue, expecting the locals to do the adjusting, limiting the communicator and perpetuating a unicultural experience.

Once individuals have more interest in speaking a foreign language, they may enroll in beginning language courses. Basic vocabulary is introduced, and the student quickly learns phrases and expressions. Also of interest are culture and customs as part of using the new language. These speakers are eager to interact with others who speak the foreign language, hoping to gain experience and practice. As long as things run smoothly, continuing in the foreign language feels comfortable and effective, but when the responses of the locals are not understood well enough to continue in the foreign language, the inexperienced speakers often apologetically revert back to their own language. New speakers realize the value of using the language but are not yet proficient enough to interact without having or wanting to use the language that is most familiar.

Individuals who have had the opportunity to learn and practice a foreign language may reach fluency, demonstrating competence. Competent speakers of a foreign language are not only able to interact on a superficial level, accomplishing daily routines like grocery shopping, ordering in a restaurant, and asking directions, but they are also able to form meaningful relationships with others in the new language, understand complex explanations, and express thoughts and feelings. It is not necessary for competent speakers to translate internally while they are speaking or listening. New ideas can be developed in the new language, and these individuals understand the nuances of culture and can translate between languages for others.

The process is similar for counselors and counselor trainees when they are introduced to strength-centered principles and language. In environments that depend on deficit-based language, practitioners may have little interest in going beyond the boundaries of the language of clinical assessments and diagnoses. Beyond interactions with clients, these counselors continue to communicate using deficit-based language with other mental health professionals, and language is used to perpetuate a focus on deficits and illness.

Counselors newly introduced to strength-centered counseling may understand the value of the principles and of using strength-centered language but have not yet gained enough training and experience to have become proficient. Just as with the individual struggling to use a newly learned foreign language, counselors new to strength-centered vocabulary feel comfortable using this language and techniques with clients, so long as sessions run along familiar, practiced lines. Yet, when counselors encounter unexpected situations, they may find themselves scurrying back to familiar habits, refocusing on deficits and perhaps undoing progress that has been made.

Strength-centered counselors who have gained competence in using strength-centered language are able to shift their focus to possibilities without denying the opportunities for growth within a client's presenting problem, and in doing so they encourage equitable relationships with clients. They are confident using strength-centered language during sessions and are able to adjust when unexpected interactions take place, maintaining a focus on strengths and resiliency. Moreover, these counselors utilize a strength stance when communicating with other mental health professionals and not only have mastered a vocabulary of strengths, but also understand the culture of strength-centered counseling, utilizing strength-centered language in their personal lives.

DIALECTICS OF PATHOLOGY AND POSSIBILITY

Incorporating a strength-centered vocabulary into practice with clients begins with recognizing the dialectical nature of pathology and possibilities. During therapeutic interactions, clients and counselors create the reality of possibilities in the face of pathology through the understanding and the acceptance that pathology and possibilities reside simultaneously within the struggle. Clients often enter counseling wanting relief from their hopelessness, and at the same time may struggle against well-meaning efforts on their behalf, and while they may experience a sense of despair, clients still possess the strengths and resources needed to go beyond only immediate relief of their suffering (see Table 4.1). A strength-centered language in counseling reflects an authentic appreciation of a client's struggle and situation along with a sincere belief that he or she can move forward because of the possibilities already present within the situation that have yet to be discovered and explored.

Table 4.1   What's Wrong and What's Strong: Pathology and Possibilities

Pathology	*Possibilities*
Problems	Solutions
The presenting problem is often the initial focus of traditional counseling sessions. Clients enter counseling because something is going wrong.	Presenting problems are at the same time the solutions clients have found in order to cope with difficult situations in their lives.
Deficits	Strengths
Maladaptive functioning, due to what individuals are missing in their lives, prevents reaching desired goals, having satisfying relationships, and developing internal satisfaction.	Commitments of personal, physical, and spiritual survival representing character virtues, confront threats to psychological well-being, and allow individuals to stand up to adversity.
Resistance	Anticipation
Clients may reject efforts on their behalf or may seem to avoid full participation in their own treatment.	Counselors and clients collaborate in defining a client's anticipated outcomes, offering clients a greater sense of balance as counseling expectations are realized.

(Continued)

Table 4.1 (Continued)

Pathology	Possibilities
Illness ←	→ **Wellness**
The medical model of counseling translates the presence of symptoms as a client's battle with illness and defines mental heath as the absence of symptoms.	More than merely the absence of symptoms, wellness goes beyond the relief of suffering and includes the addition of hoped-for outcomes that reflect a client's life preferences.
Despair ←	→ **Hope**
Inability to recognize resources and strengths already present within themselves and their situations keeps clients surrounded by feelings of despair and fosters instead an environment that supports a lack of hope.	Combining a desire for change with strengths and resources offers clients the hope that they will achieve counseling goals.
Diagnosis ←	→ **Understanding**
Categorizing individuals through examination of symptom clusters offers a name for what is going wrong in a client's life.	Each individual experiences his or her constellation of symptoms uniquely and at the same time may find comfort in the normalization of finding language to describe his or her struggle.
Treatment ←	→ **Preferences**
Prescribed courses of action coordinated with a client's diagnosis offer structure for therapy as well as highlight the expert position of the counselor, undermining the uniqueness of the client.	Guided by past interactions with clients, recognizing the preferences and values present in the client's struggle supports carrying out individualized action plans with each client.

When counselors understand how a shift in language can instill hope, elicit strengths, and recognize preferences, the connection between language and reality in creating meaning is apparent. As counseling shifts from pathology to a focus on possibilities present in a client's struggle, the client experiences a new reality. This alternative reality further influences the choice of future language, and the new reality is reinforced.

INCORPORATING A STRENGTH-CENTERED VOCABULARY

Beyond understanding the dialectics of pathology and possibilities as a theoretical foundation for using a strength-centered vocabulary, counselors new to this perspective may find themselves literally at a loss for words. One option, as with learning a foreign language, is to start with basic vocabulary and simple phrases. In the next sections, we include examples of strength-centered wording for interactions with clients. As you work through the three phases of strength-centered counseling, we suggest that you initially work from the specific wording given in each of the examples as you practice with a learning partner. At first this may feel unnatural, just as with learning a foreign language, but as you try this vocabulary on for size, you will find that these words and phrases will slip into your style of speaking. With practice you will hear your own voice speaking from a strength-centered perspective.

> The most difficult part of the strength-centered approach for me has been the language. At the same time, using language and questions as interventions seems like a basic skill that every counselor should be required to master. I'm glad that, during my last class at OU, I was actually challenged and given direction on how to master this skill! For example, I've noticed how saying "the anxiety" rather than "your anxiety" makes the anxiety a less burdensome thing to discuss. My favorite suggestion, though, has been to use "how" rather than "why" or "what" when asking a question. This tends to result in an answer that is more focused on the person's processing/perception of the problem rather than just the content/story. –Marc R.

In addition to understanding the dialectic pairs and their influence on language choice and adopting specific strength vocabulary and phrases, familiarity with a wide range of specific strengths is useful. With a broad understanding of strengths, strength-centered counselors authentically identify and reflect the strengths and resources present in clients, even for those whose only visible strength may be surviving. An extensive list of strengths and strength categories has most specifically been developed from the work Christopher Peterson and Martin Seligman (2004) within the growing field of positive psychology.

Positive Psychology

Positive psychology studies mental health (as opposed to mental illness) and the well-being of individuals, focusing on positive emotions, positive character traits, and the influence of positive institutions within society (Seligman & Csikszentmihalyi, 2000). The field of positive psychology has gathered momentum in studying interventions that go beyond the repair of damage in individuals to the building of these positive qualities and character strengths as protection against future difficulties (Snyder & Lopez, 2002). Positive psychology is as interested in the strengths of individuals as in the weaknesses. From this interest, researchers have strived to discover common strengths appreciated by human beings in relation to living in communities and across languages, ages, and cultures (Biswas-Diener, 2006; Peterson & Park, 2006; Peterson, Park, & Seligman, 2005). Duckworth, Steen, and Seligman (2005) stated that even individuals with the weightiest psychological difficulties want more than just relief of their symptoms.

Much of the research conducted under the umbrella of positive psychology is in identifying a schema for categorizing strengths. In their attempt to provide a common vocabulary to describe and work with human strengths, Peterson and Seligman (2004), in their book *Character Strengths and Virtues*, compiled a list of criteria by which a strength could be judged to measure human character qualities.

The result is a classification of 24 character strengths that exemplify six overarching virtues endorsed by many cultures across the world: wisdom, courage, humanity, justice, temperance, and transcendence (Biswas-Diener, 2006; Peterson & Park, 2006; Peterson, Park, & Seligman, 2005; Shimai et al., 2006). To be included in the classification, each strength was judged to be (a) contributing to individual fulfillment, (b) morally valued, (c) nondiminishing to others, (d) trait-like and measurable, and (e) distinctive from and deliberately cultivated through societal practices and rituals (Peterson, Park, & Seligman, 2004). When working with clients from a strength-centered perspective, it is useful for counselors not only to understand the broad categories of strengths but also to be able to identify, name, and reflect the specific strengths recognized in their clients. The following are descriptions of these broad strength categories as presented by Peterson and Seligman (2004) in their book, *Character Strengths and Virtues: A Handbook and Classification*.

Strengths of Wisdom and Knowledge

Strengths of wisdom and knowledge are cognitive traits demonstrated and internalized by individuals related to their interest in and ability to obtain and use information. This category is revealed by individuals through five specific strengths: creativity, curiosity, judgment and open-mindedness, love of learning, and perspective. *Creativity* not only is related to artistic endeavors, but also includes original thinking and ingenuity in accomplishing tasks. Curious individuals are fascinated with discovery as its own goal and ask questions in order to gain more information. Exercising good *judgment* while remaining *open-minded* relies on examining solid evidence in order to make decisions and on avoiding jumping to conclusions. Individuals experience *love of learning* as a sense of enjoyment in mastering new skills and bodies of knowledge, and demonstrating *perspective* comes from making sense of one's past experiences in order to see the world from different points of view for guiding one's own future decisions and providing counsel to others.

Strengths of Courage

Strengths of courage reflect an emotional commitment to accomplishing goals in the face of opposition through exercising a sense of will. Courage is exhibited through acts of bravery, perseverance, and honesty, and by exhibiting a zest for life. *Bravery* or valor is the ability to stand up to a threat or challenge, physical or emotional; speak up for one's beliefs; and act on convictions, even if unpopular. Following through on a task and taking pleasure in its completion, in spite of unexpected obstacles, demonstrate *perseverance*. Authentic integrity, presenting oneself sincerely, and taking responsibility for one's own actions are a testament to one's *honesty*. When doing things with full commitment, enthusiasm, and vitality, individuals show a *zest* for life.

Strengths of Humanity and Love

Our connections to others are enhanced through strengths of humanity and love. Caring for others and nurturing friendships involve the interpersonal strengths present in the capacity to love and be loved, kindness, and social intelligence. Interest in developing close, reciprocal relationships with other people is the most basic aspect of having the *capacity to love and be loved*. *Kindness* (e.g., generosity, nurturance, care, compassion, altruistic love, "niceness") is demonstrated by helping other people, wanting to care for others, and wanting to do good deeds for others and in society. Individuals who demonstrate *social intelligence* (e.g., emotional intelligence, personal intelligence) fit into various social situations through an awareness of their own and others' motives and feelings.

Strengths of Justice

Teamwork, fairness, and leadership are civic strengths that support healthy community life. Within a community, an individual who does good works with others toward group and community goals while remaining loyal to the group and those goals demonstrates *teamwork* (e.g., citizenship, social responsibility, loyalty). Treating all people according to the same standards of justice without allowing personal feelings to bias decisions underscores an individual's sense of *fairness*. Within groups, *leadership* emerges when one is effective at encouraging others to get things done and at the same time is able to maintain good relationships between group members.

Strengths of Temperance

As far back as the first century BCE, temperance has been hailed as something to be achieved. Roman philosopher Cicero suggested, "Never go to excess, but let moderation be your guide." The strengths in this category are focused on avoiding extremes in thoughts and actions in reference to ourselves and to others. Strengths of temperance include forgiveness and mercy, modesty and humility, prudence, and self-regulation. *Forgiveness and mercy* is the ability to give others a second chance and accept others' shortcomings, to let go of resentment of those who have wronged us. *Modesty and humility* is avoiding bragging, letting accomplishments speak for themselves. Individuals who make considered choices, avoiding words and actions that may be regretted later, exercise *prudence*. *Self-regulation* is exercising awareness and discipline of emotions and their resulting actions.

Strengths of Transcendence

We use strengths of transcendence to make connections between ourselves and the world around us, enhancing a sense of purpose in life. An *appreciation of beauty and excellence* is demonstrated both through simple actions like noticing one's surroundings and appreciating simple elegance, and feeling a sense of wonder about the complexity of living life. A sense of *gratitude* aids us in transcending ourselves in connection with the larger world through recognizing the good things that happen to us without taking them for granted. Feeling *hope* preserves a sense of our place in the world, allowing for optimism and future-mindedness. Maintaining a good sense of *humor* encourages playfulness and lightheartedness, bringing positive feelings and laughter to oneself and others. Strong and coherent beliefs about the larger scheme of life and one's place demonstrate *religiousness and spirituality,* which offer comfort and an articulated philosophy for living.

The overall understanding of these categories prepares strength-centered counselors to recognize individual strengths first in themselves and then in their clients. Authentic reflection of clients' strengths in session allows clients to recognize that strengths are already present in themselves. This shift in language reveals a shift in the cocreated reality between a strength-centered counselor and a client from problem to possibility and from adversity to opportunity. Throughout our discussion of the strength-centered counseling phases in later sections of this book, specific examples of strength-centered wording for eliciting and reflecting strengths are offered that can be used in practice with learning partners, with other mental health professionals, and in working with clients.

> The first night in class we were to speak of a strength we hoped that others would discover about us during our time together. I wanted to joke and say that I sing quite well. I never regarded my natural creative and artistic talents as a strength. I saw them as a mere hobby. . . . After completing the strength questionnaire, I was surprised to learn that my appreciation for beauty is viewed as a strength . . . and that was really impressive for me to hear. It was as if another whole room in this mysterious life was opened up for me—one where my natural abilities can not only be regarded, but regarded as a strength.
> –Sophia T.

PROFESSIONAL GROWTH ACTIVITY: DIALECTICAL NATURE OF PATHOLOGY AND POSSIBILITIES

This exercise is intended to help you become acquainted with the idea that strength-centered counselors are able to use language to shift the focus of a session with a client from the presenting problem to possibilities inherent in the struggle. With a learning partner share a recent struggle that has occupied your thoughts. Working through the chart *What's Wrong AND What's Strong* (see Table 4.1), consider the effect of language within each of the dialectic categories:

- Problem ◄——► Solution:

  How might you look at your struggle as a problem versus a solution?

- Deficits ◄——► Strengths:

  How might your struggle demonstrate deficits versus strengths?

- Resistance ◄——► Anticipation:

  How might you differentiate resistance against resolving your struggle versus anticipation for working through your struggle?

- Despair ◄——► Hope:

   How does your struggle bring about feelings of despair versus offer opportunities for hope?

- Illness ◄——► Wellness:

   How does your struggle present itself as illness in your life versus the levels of wellness you would like to see instead?

- Diagnosis ◄——► Understanding:

   How might naming your struggle with a diagnosis versus gaining a sense of understanding provide a level of comfort?

- Treatment ◄——► Preferences:

   How might the resolution of your struggle be affected by having a prescribed treatment versus a collaborated set of preferences?

PROFESSIONAL GROWTH ACTIVITY: STRENGTH AWARENESS

With a learning partner, have a shared conversation about the following questions, for each of you. Afterward, talk about the experience. This activity will help you recognize strengths you already possess and offer you practice at recognizing strengths in others.

- What are the best things about you?
- What is your guess about how they were developed?
- When are they most useful for you? When are they not? How come?

Join with another dyad and share your reactions to this experience.

PROFESSIONAL GROWTH ACTIVITY: STRENGTH LANGUAGE REFLECTIONS

This exercise is meant to offer practice in recognizing and intervening in order to shift a counseling dialogue from one of problems and deficits to one of preferences, values, and strengths. Practice shifting the focus from the problem as the person to the problems as a preference and a value by shifting your language. Work in a group of three, rotating with your learning partners: one member of the group should share a *problem* story. Another member of the group should briefly reflect the *problem* and what the problem implies about the storyteller's *preferences* and *values*. The third person in your triad should work as an observer of the others, offering feedback about how the reflection of the problem as a *preference* and/or a *value* helped *separate the problem from the person.* Be sure that each member of the group has an opportunity to do the activity from all three perspectives (see Table 4.2).

Table 4.2   Strength Language Reflections

Focus	Intent
Reflecting Problems as Preferences Emphasize moving from the past (problem) to the future (want).	• "So the challenge is _____, and what you prefer is _____."
Understanding Struggles as Reflections of Value Problems imply *values* and *desires*.	• "So, you value _____ and you desire _____."
The Person Is Not the Problem, the Problem Is Separating person from problem is the essence of strength-centered counseling.	• "So, part of how you keep an upper hand on your problem is _____?"

PART II

Phases of Strength-Centered Counseling

It all depends on how we look at things, and not how they are in themselves.

–Carl Jung

Phase 1: Shared Understanding

The Stance

    An Attitude of Empathic Curiosity

    A Stance of Acceptance

    An Appreciation for Ambivalence

The Steps

    Step 1: Problem Perception

    Step 2: Struggle Perception

    Step 3: Strength Perception

    Step 4: Dichotomy Perception

    Step 5: Hope Perception

Strength Centeredness Model: Shared Understanding

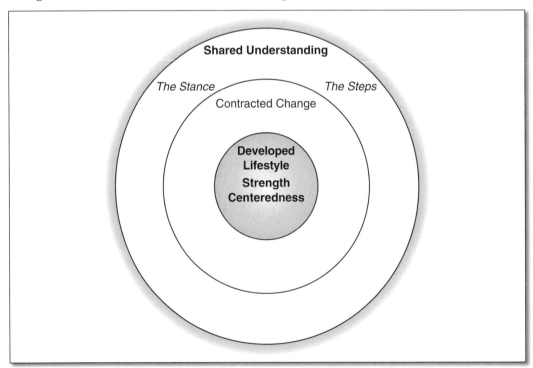

CHAPTER 5

The Stance

The paradox of reality is that no image is as compelling as the one which exists only in the mind's eye.

–Shana Alexander

As the commercial begins, a young man with long flowing hair is sitting comfortably in a leather chair located before a large stereo speaker . . . a very large stereo speaker. In a moment's flash the music begins, and as if placed in a wind tunnel, the young man's hair cascades backward while he feverishly hangs on to the chair. For new and experienced counselors alike, this can be a common professional experience when attempting to sort through the details of a client's story. People have much to say and may have waited weeks for an opportunity to say it: a retelling that progresses through a series of events often ending in a familiar feeling of hopelessness and helplessness. Clearly, individuals and families need safety and space to tell their stories. However, if the counselor seeks only to "hang on" to the chair as the client's story swiftly flows past, then a number of outcomes are likely: Although feeling heard, the client will leave with the same conclusions and emotional consequences that he or she had when entering the session; the counselor will become preoccupied with *putting the pieces of the story together,* leading to the overuse of closed-ended questions and content summaries; and when clinical listening becomes *content heavy* on facts, events, and consequences, the only available interventions are problem-solving strategies. Although these strategies may have potential benefit, if offered prematurely this teaching intervention can result in clients defending the status quo in response to a counselor's benevolent suggestions for personal change. It is far more helpful, and efficient, to build counseling relationships through *shared understanding* between the counselor and client of how problem stories are experienced rather than through what is being told.

A shared understanding results from clients experiencing a counselor's appreciation of the struggles, values, and impact the problem narrative is having in clients' lives and on their relationships. It requires counselors to engage in the process of understanding not just client problems and the stories surrounding them but also who clients are. Actively sharing the valor, loyalty, persistence, honesty, prudence, and acceptance transparent when confronting life struggles allows clients to experience their stories and themselves differently, while building a personal knowledge of unrecognized strengths necessary when considering change. The following are key counselor characteristics central to understanding the perceptions people experience around their presenting problems as well as the perceptions they have of themselves. By entering the counseling process with an *attitude of curiosity, a stance of acceptance,* and *an appreciation for ambivalence* inherent in decisions related to personal and social change, therapeutic trust is established. This is the foundation of the phases of strength-centered counseling and of the idea that people have the resources and strengths to withstand and prosper in the face of life challenges.

AN ATTITUDE OF EMPATHIC CURIOSITY

It is a miracle that curiosity survives formal education.

–Albert Einstein

Curiosity stems from the Latin root *cura,* meaning to "handle with care." It also highlights a desire to know or learn something extraordinary (*American Heritage Dictionary,* 2009). *An attitude of empathic curiosity* is a willingness to enter into and share the extraordinary world of another as well as a desire to acknowledge that which is remarkable in our clients. Consider moments in your life when you might have felt overwhelmed and remained motionless when facing struggles. In what ways might it have been helpful to have a counselor recognize and appreciate the impact of your struggles while recognizing the values, hopes, and personal strengths you brought to bear in "keeping your head above water"? *An attitude of empathic curiosity* seeks to understand a client's struggle and problems by orienting toward the strengths, hopes, values, emotion, and remarkable personal qualities emergent from lives struggling "for something different." From a strength-centered perspective, every struggle and each problem presented in counseling implies personal strengths about the client and the efforts in standing up to adversity. These strengths are not affirmations or wishful thinking, because this would be more about the counselor's need to comfort than the client's need to be comforted. Strength reflections are accurate representations of those qualities and characteristics inherent in every struggle to "right the ship" and "keep our heads above water" that go unnoticed due to the noise and urgency of the storm. It is the noise and urgency of life's storms that can narrow perception and quickly generate a cycle where fear begets fear and the experience of anxiety serves only to highlight life's worries. White and Epston (1990) described this pattern as a "problem-saturated" life where individuals perceive, anticipate, and act on only those experiences consistent with their personal "narratives."

An *attitude of empathic curiosity* demonstrated by counselors toward clients can serve to widen the perceptual window of others and provide opportunities for the inclusion of unrecognized and omitted experiences highlighting personal strengths and resilient efforts. For a better understanding of the counseling stance of *empathic curiosity* and how it informs the strength-centered counselor, think of a recent personal struggle. As if you are the counselor, reflect on each guiding question below, and respond as if you are the client. Make note of your experience, and share your reactions in your journal or with a learning partner:

- What does your struggle imply about your values, your hopes?
- What beliefs about yourself, others, and the world around you are being challenged or possibly compromised as you reflect on your struggle?
- What does it mean to you to have this struggle?
- What have you learned about yourself? How have you sustained yourself in the face of this struggle?
- Referring to Table 5.1, Strength Characteristics, what personal strengths have you needed to tap into?
- What does the struggle imply about what you prefer to be different in yourself and/or in your life? What strengths will you likely need to develop in order to see this occur, even just a little?

Table 5.1	Strength Characteristics	

Categories of Strengths	Strengths
Wisdom and Knowledge Use of Knowledge	• Creativity • Curiosity • Judgment and Open-Mindedness • Love of Learning • Perspective
Courage Exercise of Will	• Bravery (Valor) • Perseverance • Honesty • Zest
Humanity and Love Befriending Others	• Capacity to Love and Be Loved • Kindness • Social Intelligence
Justice Civic Responsibility	• Teamwork • Fairness • Leadership
Temperance Protection Against Excess	• Forgiveness and Mercy • Modesty and Humility • Prudence • Self-Regulation
Transcendence and Meaning Connection to the Larger Universe	• Appreciation of Beauty and Excellence • Gratitude • Hope • Humor • Religiousness and Spirituality

Source: Adapted from Peterson and Seligman (2004).

A STANCE OF ACCEPTANCE

Yet, listening, of this very special kind, is one of the most potent forces for change that I know.

–Carl Rogers (1980)

Empathy is a willingness to let others know that you know what life might be like from their frames of experience. It embodies an *acceptance* of actions without evaluation, and the presence of ideas without judgment. Empathy provides a climate that stands in stark contrast to common interactions we have with supervisors, teachers, principals, police officers, parents, friends, and family where their "approval" is contingent on a set of behaviors or actions. Adolescents referred to counseling have been reminded often of their misbehaviors, shortcomings, and inabilities to engender adult approval. To accept others "unconditionally" is to acknowledge that people are more than just an accumulation of past behaviors and failed attempts to change (Rogers, 1957). They are defined by the strengths, resources, and characteristics learned and brought to bear against life's evolving challenges, and not by the weight of their histories. This type of listening represents a decision to *suspend* personal values in order to walk in the shoes of another and reflect back the emotions, values, and strengths *implied* in their struggle and the hopes *transparent* in the conflict.

Rarely does a parent begin a session with,

> You know, I have become acutely aware that my overreactions with my teenage daughter are actually reflections of my hopes that she will not make the same mistakes I made, and I am wondering how I might find better ways to express those values without always arguing about what I don't want and listening more to what she wants.

If only all sessions began like this! More often than not, the essence of another's experience is reflected in the *complaints*, implied in the *symptoms*, and transparent in the *expectations* illustrated within the stories brought to counseling. Below are common complaints presented by clients early in counseling. Beside each complaint is a potential strength-centered counselor response demonstrating both an empathic understanding of the problem and an acceptance of the experience and worldview of the client (see Table 5.2). Make note of how these reflective responses might have differed from your own, if you were the counselor.

The sample responses in Table 5.2 demonstrate an empathic *stance of acceptance* to the complaint, symptom, or expectation introduced by clients. Although each statement is focused on "another," the empathic reflection is focused on the client worldview and experience. With a learning partner, discuss potential reactions that counselors might have to the client expressions above and how these might hinder demonstrating empathy through *a stance of acceptance*. What might be other counselor responses that focus on the client worldview and experience?

Table 5.2	Reflected Experience: Complaint, Symptom, Expectation

Possible Client Statement Problem/Complaint	Potential Counselor Response Empathic Acceptance
Complaint "My husband has had a drinking problem for a long time. I've left him twice, and each time he stopped for a while. Things are nice between us when he isn't drinking. Recently, he said he can control his drinking, but I am afraid he's going to start up again. I don't know what to do."	"You value trusting others, but you're unsure about trusting yourself to make the right decision because you don't want to be disappointed that you might not able to trust your husband."
Symptom "I worry about my daughter all the time. I know she is 18 and needs to find her way at college, but I find myself sleeping less and less. My husband says I'm distracted and just wants me to 'let it go.' I just can't seem to stop thinking about her."	"You want your daughter to know that even though you know that she is grown up enough to be away on her own, part of you still sees her as your little girl and you want to protect her, and it's upsetting to you that your husband doesn't feel the same attachment to her."
Expectation "My family is nuts. We fight all the time. I never know what to do. I just want us not to fight so much."	"You'd like it if your family were just like happy families you see on TV, with lots of harmony and joking around. That way you'd know what to expect. It that partly it?"

AN APPRECIATION FOR AMBIVALENCE

It is never too late to be what you might have been.

–George Eliot

W. R. Miller and Rollnick (2002), in their seminal work on the tenets of Motivational Interviewing, described ambivalence as a central experience to be explored and resolved when discussing behavior changes with clients. Ambivalence is perceived as a normal reaction to the human experience when balancing "the need to do something different" with "the benefits of doing more of the same." Anyone who has sought to change an aspect of his or her lifestyle (e.g., smoking, weight loss, exercise) knows this inner dialogue well. It is not the absence of ambivalence that embodies motivation, but the presence of it. This often flies in the face of traditional addiction models that perceive ambivalence as the "door to relapse" and a "red flag" signaling a lack of motivation, illustrative of resistance. It is consistent with a two-dimensional life perspective where change either occurs or it does not. This perception can be heard in the experience of clients and families as they describe a reluctance to sacrifice the known for the unknown, the resignation that change is hopeless, the rebellion that change would be a "giving in" to another's demand, and/or rationalization of how change, although needed, is unlikely given the current status of things. Offering suggestions, albeit benevolent, only parallels this perspective and can quickly lead to a "yes, but" conversation and continued feelings of hopelessness and helplessness for both clients and counselors. To experience this more fully, attempt the activity below with a learning partner. Afterward, reflect on how this pattern emerges in your relationships.

Activity: Benevolent Suggestions

Person A *(A voice warning against change)*

Express a current life dilemma to your partner. When offered a suggestion, respond with, "Yes, but . . ." and continue your explanation.

Person B *(A voice for change)*

Listen and respond empathically. When ready, provide a benevolent suggestion with reasons why this would be helpful for your partner.

Person A responds to suggestion with, "Yes, but . . ."

Person B listens empathically and provides an additional suggestion.

Repeat this for process for 8 to 10 minutes

Trade roles; reflect on the experience

This type of interchange can occur in almost any relationship and, as you experienced above, can leave both parties frustrated. This is often illustrated in counselors who conclude that clients are *resistant* or *noncompliant* with treatment suggestions, and clients that feel misunderstood and discounted regarding the complexities of their lives. It is the responsibility of strength-centered counselors, and not the clients they serve, to promote a *shared understanding*. Therefore, it is important to resist the "righting response" where the counselor directly or implicitly takes up the "positive side" of change. A pro-change stance by the counselor often leaves folks in the unenviable position of defending the status quo—whether they want to or not. Normalizing and recognizing the inherent ambivalence associated with life struggles provides a window to better understanding personal difficulties associated with change. It also provides recognition of the complexities and the multidimensional views of the human experience.

PROFESSIONAL GROWTH ACTIVITY: THE COMPLEXITIES OF CHANGE

In a small group (three or four) decide on one member who will sit on the floor while the others stand. Make note of the following instructions and the process questions following the experience.

- *Instructions for the sitting individual:* You have good reasons for sitting. Although you consider standing at times, and others have encouraged you to, the thought of it seems overwhelming at times. For now, you have decided to sit.
- *Instructions for those standing:* You each have good reasons to get the person sitting to stand. Not only are you evaluated on your success to get folks to stand, but you also have limited time. Without the use of physical force, your work as a team is somehow to get the person sitting on the floor to stand.
- *Process Questions:*

  - What was this experience like for the "sitters"? For the "standers"?
  - What strategies were utilized by the standers? Which proved to be helpful and which did not? Do you utilize any of these strategies in work with people now? How come?
  - For those sitting, of the strategies utilized by your peers, which proved to be most helpful? Which were not? How would you describe your struggle between sitting and the possible desire to stand? How might this be similar in your own life or the lives of those you work with?

COUNSELOR INTERVIEW & REFLECTION GUIDE

Shared Understanding: The Stance

Focus	Intervention
Shared Understanding An Attitude of Curiosity	*Professional Reflection Questions for the Counselor* What does the struggle imply about the values and hopes of the client? What client beliefs are being challenged or possibly compromised in the face of the struggles? What does it mean for the client to have this struggle? What are clients learning about themselves? How have they sustained themselves in facing the struggle? What personal strengths have they needed to tap into? (See Table 5.2, Strength Characteristics) What does their struggle imply about what they would prefer different in themselves or in their lives? What strengths will likely need to be developed in order to see this occur, even just a little?
A Stance of Acceptance	*Professional Reflection Questions for the Counselor* Do the clients know that you know the essence of their experience reflected in the complaints, implied in the symptoms, and transparent in the expectations illustrated within their narrative? What are the emotions, values, and strengths implied in the struggle and the hopes transparent in the conflict?

(Continued)

(Continued)

Focus	Intervention
Ambivalence Appreciation	What does his or her struggle with others tell you about the client? Does he or she know that you know? *Ambivalence (Explanation Models) Questions for the Client* "What is your theory about why change has been difficult for you?" "How have you tried to solve this and why have those efforts proved unsuccessful up until now?" "So, the problem is _____ and what you want is _____." *Ambivalence (Change Models) Questions for the Client* "In what ways would it be good for you to (action)?" "If you did decide to change, how would you do it? What would be your reasons for doing something different?" "What are the good things about change and what are the not-so-good things?"

The Steps

The mere relief of suffering does not lead to well-being; it only removes one of the barriers to well-being.

–Duckworth, Steen, & Seligman (2005)

There is a story of a man who, upon finding an emperor moth struggling to force itself through a small hole, kindly cut away the cocoon to ease the emergence of the moth. What he failed to realize in his haste to be helpful, was how the struggle to free itself from the cocoon provided the moth needed fluids to be forced into its wings. Only then would the moth be prepared to fly. Without the struggle, as the man witnessed, the moth would never be able to fly. So it is with strength-centered counseling. Understanding how individuals have been "stretched" by life's struggles as well as those resilient attributes necessary in one's fight for personal freedom is the essence of strength-centered counseling and developing a shared understanding of the perceptions that clients and families experience in relationship to their problems and life struggles.

The following are steps designed to create an active encounter between counselors and clients that explore the perception of their concerns and the impact these concerns have on themselves and others as well as how life's struggles, and the strengths therein, inform their perceptions of hope for a better future. People are far more than the problems they struggle against, and the 5 steps essential to this phase of strength-centered counseling seek to highlight this distinction. Although presented below in a linear fashion, the steps toward this goal are often dynamic and unique to the emergent qualities between counselors and clients.

STEP 1: PROBLEM PERCEPTION

It is one of the commonest of mistakes to consider that the limit of our power of perception is also the limit of all there is to perceive.

–C. W. Leadbeater

At its core, the helping relationship is an action of courage: the courage of the counselor to accept, support, and invite others in self-discovery, and the courage of clients to accept the warmth and care of an "empathic stranger" while exploring the impact and influence life problems are having on themselves and others. During this segment in developing *a shared understanding,* the emphasis is on gathering a fuller appreciation regarding how clients are experiencing their problems and initial concerns. Below are questions designed to engage counselors in understanding the relationship clients have with their problems (see Table 6.1). Although regarded as clinical interventions, these questions are still only a guide and cannot replace the emergent quality of an empathic dialogue between clients and counselors. They seek only to engage both parties in understanding the impact and influence these problems have on clients' lives as well as their expectations for counseling. This step provides a foundation for appreciating the distinction between life problems and the unique qualities of individuals and families struggling for "better lives," which will be further explored in later segments of this phase of strength-centered counseling.

Table 6.1	Problem Perception Questions	

Problem Perception	Problem Impact	Problem Influence
"Can you think of a name to call this problem? What is it like (picture/metaphor)?" "What is your theory about why this is a problem?" "Are there other problems that this teams up with? In what ways does it do this?"	"What impact has the problem had on you/others?" "How has the problem robbed you of what you want?" "How does the problem 'get the best of you'? What has it promised you?" "What do you think will happen if you do not make a change?"	"Would the problem want you in counseling? How did it try to keep you from coming?" "What does the problem whisper in your ear?" "How much of your life does it control? Is this your preferred way of being or would you prefer something else?" "Who else might be an advocate with you in standing up to the influence of the problem?"

Mosaic art is just like life. There are pieces put together and pieces broken. Life is the same, the pieces are like stages in life, and the broken pieces are like calamities. Although they are broken and torn, if glued together they are a piece of beautiful artwork. In life if we can appreciate the meaning of the so-called negative events, we will realize that our life is as beautiful and multifaceted as a mosaic art. –Lila Y.

People often enter counseling fatigued with a weariness resulting from the tireless efforts in managing life's stress and challenges. This constant exertion can impact concentration, mood, and our ability to fight off disease as well as cope with unforeseen occurrences. From a strength-centered perspective, this fatigue is a statement about the difficulty of the climb and not the climber. It is not an estimation of an individual's level of functioning in terms of presenting problems and personal deficits, but rather, an understanding of those strengths and resources utilized by individuals in their struggle against problems and personal deficits. Although this can be contrary to the training many counselors experience, Tallman and Bohart (1999), in their review of therapy outcome studies, remind us that clients, and not counselors, are the primary agents of therapeutic change.

Eliciting a dialogue with clients about the explanations as to why problems have persisted, their expectations for counseling, and the difficulties of change can be very useful in better understanding the ambivalence embedded in their struggle for personal and familial change. Client explanatory models can provide a very important window into the personal meaning, values, and culture associated with the difficulties faced when considering "something different." Furthermore, clarifying the expectations that clients have of counseling, and the counselor, assists with highlighting the fundamental purpose of counseling: client-directed change. This can be enhanced by eliciting a conversation with others on the process of change . . . beyond just the target of change. The following strategic questions are designed to elicit *shared understanding* of the struggle between one's hope for change and the difficulties that change represents (see Table 6.2) as well as add to the problem perception of clients and families.

Table 6.2 Expanded Perception of the Problem

Exploring Explanations	Identifying Expectations	Eliciting a Change Conversation
"What is your theory about why change has been difficult for you?"	"When things are more on track, what will be different in you as well as in your life?"	"In what ways would it be good for you to change or 'do something different'?"
"How have you tried to solve this and why have your efforts proved unsuccessful up until now?"	"How will you know when counseling is no longer necessary?"	"If you did decide to change, how would you do it? What would be your reasons for doing something different?"
"So, the problem is _____ and what you want is _____.		"What are the good things about change and what are the not so good things?"

STEP 2: STRUGGLE PERCEPTION

The strongest have their moments of fatigue.

–Friedrich Nietzsche

John Wesley Powell (1875/1987), in his exploration of the Grand Canyon, expressed that the immense canyon could not be seen from just one view and that it required a perspective from many sides and seasons to gain a full appreciation. In much the same way, strength-centered counselors believe that people have the capacity to explore other sides of an experience. Whereas beauty is meaningless without an understanding of ugliness, hopelessness can best be understood by knowing what hope is, and sorrow is itself defined by happiness. From this perspective, individuals can be encouraged to rise above a struggle and to perceive it from many angles, resulting in the appreciation of what the struggle can offer rather than running from or denying it. During this clinical encounter the problem and solution are viewed as different sides of the same coin, rather than separate currencies. As Weick and Chamberlain (2002) theorized, clients who feel they have been intentionally validated achieve their counseling goals at a higher rate than those who feel they have not been so validated by their counselors. As helping professionals, we often estimate clients' levels of functioning primarily in terms of their deficits rather than in terms of their strengths.

> Through this experience I have learned that sometimes as a counselor we are going to have to work with what we've got, and that means identifying what strengths the clients currently have that can help them through their current situations. It is not like teaching them a new technique because they already have the knowledge and skills to use the strengths. As counselors it is our job to help them tap into those strengths, bring them into their current reality and explore with them how to apply them now to their current situations. –Garrett S.

The suggestions below can assist clients and families with exploring presenting problems with an emphasis on the struggle and those strengths inherent therein. This emphasis is grounded in the clinical belief that where there are deficits, there are strengths; where problems arise, there are preferences; where there is resistance, there is also anticipation; where there is illness, there are opportunities for wellness; and where despair resides, hope lives also. To elicit this kind of counseling interchange is to provide others with the idea that they are more than that which they struggle against. It is a shared understanding of the struggle and resilient qualities that have maintained their spirits in the face of adversity.

Table 6.3	Strengths Within the Struggle	

"With all that you are managing right now, it makes complete sense you are tired and depressed. Your fatigue is likely more about the load you are carrying than about you. In fact, I am a bit surprised that things haven't become worse. How have you *managed* to keep your head above water?"

"Talk about those qualities you have *learned* about yourself that assist in sustaining yourself in the face of stress. What would *others* say about the qualities that you have that keep you going during these periods?"

"What *advice* do you give to yourself that helps to keep your head above water and reminds you to keep moving forward?"

"When was the last time you felt *hopeful* about your life and circumstances? What was going on in your life that made you feel hopeful?"

As the client responds to these open-ended questions, a strength-centered counselor listens for and reflects the client's strengths and resources (see Table 6.3). With follow-up questions and reflections the counselor also elicits from the client his or her own identification and recognition of these and other strengths as they are demonstrated within the struggle. In the following dialog, notice the inclusion of language that elicits from the client her strengths within the struggle:

Client: I decided to come in today because I just have a lot of anxiety I'm trying to deal with. I'm just really anxious all the time. I'm having trouble sleeping, crying a lot. I just don't know what to do.

Counselor: It sounds like it's had a huge impact on your life.

Client: Yeah, it's huge, and it's just getting really bad. Like the last year, I just don't know what to do to try and control it.

Counselor: A year, that's a long time to deal with something like that. *How do you manage to keep going every day?*

Client: Well, I don't know. Some days it's harder than others. When I have my son there, it's okay. At least it's the reason to get up, and that's my motivation, but when he's not there, I don't really have a reason.

Counselor: So being there for your son sounds like an inspiration for you to do what you need do during the day.

Client: Yeah, it is. It's really important, but his dad just controls everything, and that's what makes it so hard. He's always controlled everything. You know, I married him when I was nineteen, but I left him a few years ago. Still, he always controls everything with our son, and it's making me crazy.

Counselor: You're feeling a bit helpless in the situation.

Client: I do. I feel really helpless. I don't know what to do, and I'm trying to get trained in cosmetology, so I can get something going for myself.

Counselor: So how do you handle the anxiety? *How have you managed to keep your head above water?*

Client: This is a huge step, even coming to see you. I talked to my best friend, and he didn't want me to come in to see you. The thing is, I'm not handling it well.

Counselor: You did come here, and you are taking care of your son when you're able to see him. And you're starting to take control over some things, like looking into schooling options.

Client: Yes, but these aren't getting me where I want to be.

Counselor: Where do you want to be?

Client: Away from my ex-husband. He's just trouble. He's a problem. He manipulates the situation to get what he wants. He came to take me shopping with my son, but he doesn't give anything without wanting something in return. And I don't want to give him anything. I'm tired of him. I'm tired of what he does, but I've got to see my son.

Counselor: Getting here is a huge first step, and I commend you for that. It takes a lot of courage to do that, especially going against the wishes of someone who you obviously seek support from. *What advice do you give yourself to keep moving forward?*

Client: I don't know. I just wonder what's the point? Except for Jason. I just want to be there for my son.

Counselor: You've talked about the other people in your life, and I get the sense that you feel they are controlling you with your son. You're feeling forced into a situation. This is a lot for anybody to go through. *It makes sense that you have so much stress and anxiety, feeling like you have no control, like you're at the mercy of other people. It's a challenge.*

Client: You're right, it is. It's a challenge.

As witnessed above, through the use of strategic open-ended questions and strength-related counselor responses, the client begins to explore another side of her life events. She begins to see herself working to be a good mother to her son within the struggle to gain time with him. Her stress and anxiety are about this noble commitment. To obtain a shared understanding of the struggle of others is to open a window to unrecognized strengths and personal values.

> For me, strength-centered counseling offered a change in language. At the time I was introduced to strength-centered techniques I was struggling to really identify with a counseling approach. There were bits and pieces from several theories that I felt comfortable with, but there was something missing, and this filled in the gap. From the moment I was introduced to this technique it felt natural, and I remember thinking how I'd wished I had been exposed to it sooner. This approach shaped my basic communication with clients by providing a way to better offer hope simply by utilizing their own life experiences. While working with clients in an inpatient drug and alcohol rehabilitation center, I found strength-centered counseling techniques especially valuable. These clients are at such a low point in their lives, some of them feel getting through the day is too overwhelming, and they cannot imagine the next few weeks of recovery. Instilling hope is vital, and what better way to do that than using clients' own lives and their experiences to relate to ways they have overcome obstacles in their pasts? It seems as though people are not aware of their strengths and how they use them in their day-to-day lives. I think if I can help clients realize that despite their current feelings about themselves, they are capable of making changes, then I have fulfilled my role as a counselor. –Cassandra S.

STEP 3: STRENGTH PERCEPTION

People develop strengths as part of their driving force to meet basic psychological needs,
such as belonging and affiliation, competency, feeling safe, autonomy, and/or finding
meaning and purpose in life.

–Richard M. Ryan and Edward L. Deci (2000)

Lent (2004) argued that counseling can be conceptualized as an enterprise that is designed to restore and/or promote well-being. By focusing on the struggle against daily problems, rather than just the problem and/or solution itself, the dynamic qualities of personal resiliency can be explored. Within these efforts of resiliency are strength attributes that can be understood and utilized by clients in seeking symptom relief as well as a restoration of life satisfaction. Resilience, then, is a process of strength development. As introduced in Chapter 4, Table 6.4 illustrates the dynamic relationship between patterns of resilience and strength development.

Table 6.4 Patterns of Resilience and Strength Development		
Themes of Resiliency: *Adversity Experiences* *(Wagnild & Young, 1990)*	*Characteristics of Strengths:* *Life Experiences* *(Peterson & Seligman, 2004)*	*Strength Qualities:* *Developed Characteristics*
EQUANIMITY (Life Perspective)	WISDOM AND KNOWLEDGE (Use of Knowledge)	Creativity, Curiosity, Open-Mindedness, Learning, Perspective
PERSEVERANCE (Tenacity)	COURAGE (Exercise of Will)	Valor, Persistence, Integrity, Honesty, Responsible, Vitality
SELF-RELIANCE (Self-Efficacy)	HUMANITY AND LOVE (Befriending Others)	Caring, Kindness, Generosity, Social Intelligence, Empathy
EXISTENTIAL ALONENESS (Uniqueness)	JUSTICE (Civic Responsibility)	Loyalty, Teamwork, Fairness, Leadership, Organizing, Decisive
HARDINESS (Strength Awareness)	TEMPERANCE (Protect Against Excess)	Forgiveness, Humility, Accepting, Prudence, Cautious, Disciplined
MEANINGFULNESS (Opportunities)	TRANSCENDENCE (Connection to the Larger Universe)	Appreciative, Grateful, Hopeful, Faithful, Optimistic, Playful, Spiritual

Because strengths are recognized to be malleable and changeable as well as learned and taught (Benson, Galbraith, & Espeland, 1995), the recognition of strengths within the resilient efforts presented by clients can have a healing effect. Counseling that recognizes and elicits those strengths inherent in the struggle helps clients to manage stress, cope with adversity, and increase their satisfaction in themselves and others.

One of the tenets of strength-centered counseling is that the more we worry about problems, the more we notice when they happen rather than noticing when they happen less. As a strength-centered counselor, to assist the client in homing in on those little successes empowers him [or her] to stay in the trenches despite the difficulty. To elicit strengths from the client from these successes gives the client the confidence to do more. How refreshing for clients to hear more than trite compliments but genuine strengths pulled from their own struggles.
–Maureen C.

Strength questions are designed to elicit personal qualities often hidden by misery, protective strategies, and the failure to achieve goals set by others. They are designed to shift the clinical focus toward the unique attributes of clients/families distinct from their life challenges. This is often uncomfortable (for both clients and counselors) and requires patience from the counselor as strengths are verbalized and explored. Although recognizing the strength characteristics (see Table 5.1, Strength Characteristics, in Chapter 5) can be useful, appreciating the hesitancy that accompanies the expression of personal strengths is essential. Whether social, cultural, or familial in cause, it is far easier to articulate what is lacking than what is abundant. The expression of what is "going wrong" often overshadows that which is "going right," and the urge to focus on the experience of others distracts from a focus inward. To experience this more fully, attempt the learning activity below and reflect on your emotional experience as well as your reasons why.

Activity: My Strengths

With a learning partner, have a shared dialogue around the following focus questions:

1. What do you like most about yourself?

2. What might others say they appreciate about you?

3. What do you secretly hope others will discover about you?

Identifying and expressing personal strengths can be uncomfortable for many. Not only can the expression of positive personal qualities be experienced as "selfish," "boastful," and/or "arrogant," it confronts a cultural deficit language often used to describe ourselves and others. An example of this is illustrated in the supervision of counselors. If asked how their last counseling sessions went, it is not uncommon to hear a recounting of all that should have been done or said as well as the many opportunities missed to intervene differently with their clientele. Counselors are clearly not immune from the temptation to perceive efforts that fall short of their expectations as statements of personal failure. This can diminish the complexities associated with their professional growth and thwart the necessary risk-taking actions needed for increasing their professional confidence. In the spirit of the strength-centered questions above, this perspective might be shifted with supervisees by asking them to reflect on *what they learned about themselves in the counseling session that appeared to make a difference for their clients*. The discovery of inherent personal qualities that make a difference in considering "something different" is the essence of this phase of strength-centered counseling and essential in providing the foundation for future change.

Below are questions for eliciting general strengths as well as additional questions that can be used with the same intent (see Table 6.5). The anchoring questions allow clients the opportunity to link their strengths with their concerns. Providing an empathic relationship in which clients can "make sense" of their struggles in the context of their strengths, triggers hope and is the essence of this initial phase of strength-centered counseling. In other words, it is not the removal of personal deficits or the replacement of dysfunctional thoughts/behaviors that embody change, but the inclusion of personal attributes already present. "Anchoring" strengths with the problems people seek to address in counseling is fundamentally inspiring and pragmatically necessary in securing a motivational readiness for change.

Table 6.5   Eliciting and Anchoring Strengths

Eliciting General Strengths	Anchoring Strengths	Additional Questions
"What are the best things about you? What is your guess about how they were developed?" "What special characteristics or talents distinguish you from others?" "What do you wish others might discover about you?" "When are your strengths most useful for you? When are they not? What is your theory about this?"	"How might some of these attitudes, beliefs, and strengths be adapted and applied to your current difficulties?" "What strengths do you believe you need to develop to better address the difficulties we have discussed?" "How have you managed to keep things from getting worse?"	"What do you do well?" "What do other people look to you for?" "What are your outstanding qualities?" "How and with whom do you build alliances?" "How have you been able to adapt to change?" "Tell me what you do when you are at your best."

To offer clients and counselors a hands-on experience with eliciting specific strengths and strength categories, we have developed Strength Cards, which are used in a format similar to a Vocational Card Sort (Dolliver, 1967). Strength Cards elicit a client's strengths and his or her attitudes about the strengths. Clients sort a set of Strength Cards into three piles: Strengths I Have, Strengths I Don't Have, and Strengths I'm Not Sure About. Each Strength Card is printed on one side with the name of one of the strength categories (as adapted from Peterson & Seligman, 2004) and on the other with the name of a specific corresponding strength. The activity begins with the sorting of the first card. Clients usually find themselves already talking about their strengths as they are deciding into which stack to sort the card. Working with the cards has many variations beyond this described sorting. A full set of Strength Cards is included in Appendix F. Also, you may refer to our Web site, www .sagepub.com/wardreuter, for more complete explanations and a video demonstration of how to use Strength Cards with clients. Below, two counselors recount their experience using Strength Cards:

> Mary spent most of the first session slumped in her chair, arms crossed, recounting her history both in and out of treatment. As she got to the present, she described a party she had recently attended. She had enjoyed herself talking to a young man during the evening and left feeling like she had started a relationship with him. Once home, she was sure that the relationship would go nowhere. She kept replaying their conversation in her head, going over every word. What did he mean when he said x? Could there be multiple interpretations? How did he take her response to x? What might she have said instead? While ruminating about her interactions, her body language changed, she was not detached from her description. She finally looked at me straight on, as though she wanted a response, for I had been listening rather than verbally responding. I commented about her keen analytical skills and asked if there are other parts of her life where she makes good use of being able to recall so many details and their connections. She described being good at her job, something she had not yet mentioned, and having been a fairly good student when she was in school. We ended the session focused on her ability to analyze situations and relate to them.
>
> In the following sessions, we discovered many other strengths already residing within her, and we worked on helping her recognize and develop those strengths. Much of this work depended on the language we used in the sessions together. First she realized that we were partners, and that it was our responsibility to do good work together. Second, hearing authentic reflections of her strengths gave her the confidence to recognize them in herself.
>
> One activity well received by Mary was using Strength Cards. After sorting, I asked her to take the cards with her, keep them in her pocket. If she wanted to she could jot down thoughts on any of the cards during the week. A few weeks later she brought the cards with her. She found that she wanted to keep only some of the cards with her, and on those she wrote comments about when she found herself using the specific strengths. Additionally, talking about why other cards had not made it into her pocket was also interesting. She found that some were strengths that she had the opportunity to develop, rather than looking at them as things she was not able to do, again using strength-centered vocabulary. –Denita P.

> Someone brought up the idea of flipping through the Strength Cards prior to a client's appointment as a way to get tuned in to that person's strengths. I have even started doing that at home and work when I find myself challenged by a person's behavior, I flip through the cards (either physically or mentally) and select some strengths of that person. It helps to shift and expand my point of view so I can address that person more positively and the overall situation with more openness. –Daniella G.

STEP 4: DICHOTOMY PERCEPTION

The curious paradox is that when I accept myself just as I am, then I can change.

–Carl Rogers

As part of their driving force to meet basic psychological needs, people develop strengths, such as belonging and affiliation, competency, feeling safe, autonomy, and/or finding meaning and purpose in life (Ryan & Deci, 2000). From a strength-centered point of view, difficulty arises not in the pursuit of these needs but in the exclusionary use of one's unique personal strengths to meet these needs. For example, caution and restraint can be useful, especially during times of intense emotional distress; however, the dichotomy of these strengths can be indecision and missed opportunities when taking responsibility for life choices. Compassion toward the welfare of others can lead to resenting the sacrifice of personal needs. Optimism can distract from the growing influence of life problems and can lead to episodes of personal crisis. Appreciating the strengths that people bring to bear on life challenges is central to building hope and readiness for change; however, it is also important to assist clients and families with understanding how strengths, when utilized exclusively in the face of adversity, can often be "too much of a good thing" and thwart efforts toward life satisfaction and conflict resolution. To further experience this paradox, reflect on your experience with the following activity.

Activity: Dichotomy

With a learning partner, have a shared dialogue around the following focus questions:

1. What would you say are your greatest gifts as a person?

2. What is your theory on how you developed these gifts? What influenced their development?

3. How are these gifts a handicap at times? What strengths would you rather tap into instead at those times?

Strengths are reflected truths present in every struggle and presenting problem. They highlight an unrecognized commitment, by clients and counselors alike, to personal, physical, and spiritual survival. Strengths are not affirmations (a hoped-for personal truth) or simply finding positive qualities in negative experiences (false reassurance). The identification of strengths, and its dichotomy in confronting adversity, represents characteristics empathically understood by clients and counselors that confront threats to psychological well-being.

In my work with clients, I have already used some of the strength-centered approaches with one of my clients. The woman had been in an abusive situation with her boyfriend. She would talk about how she knows she should not be with him and said as much. Even though I did my best to tell her whatever she chooses, it is her choice, and to communicate that I was not judging her, she still came across in a manner that made me think she felt I was judging her. It was not until I did a reflection of her strengths of loyalty and caring qualities that this dynamic changed. I reflected how, even though she experiences a lot of difficulty in this relationship, that she a very loyal person who would stick by her partner even in the tough times. [Her guard lowered a bit.] Then, I asked if she ever felt that her loyalty got the best of her. She really broke down for the first time in eight sessions, and this led to a more honest communication about how she is always there for the people in her life and that they tend to "fall short." The client also talked about how this "bad" relationship, even though she knows it will not work out, is the last thing she is holding on to. We really had a completely different dialogue than in the previous several sessions. The conversation got to a deeper level, and the client really seemed to open up more in the process. –Julie J.

The following sequence of therapeutic statements assists individuals with recognizing their strengths and the origin of their development as well as how, even with the best intentions, these same strengths can stand in the way of efforts to overcome adversity (see Table 6.6). To illustrate this further, a brief counseling transcript is included.

Table 6.6	Dichotomy of Strengths	

Summary of strengths (see previous steps)

Discuss how, despite your best intentions, these qualities/strengths get the best of you at times. How is this true in your current struggles? What other strengths might you wish to tap into instead during these times?

Client: I feel like I've always been a person who tries really hard to stay cheerful and carefree. Sometimes it's better just to feel how I feel.

Counselor: It's hard for you, but you stay upbeat for others? *Could you share with me what has influenced you to develop into the kind of person who tries to be happy and cheerful?*

Client: I don't know. Maybe because it's just easier to be positive. I used to be very open about my feelings, but lately I'm covering up. I don't want to be seen as weak. I don't know. That might be it.

Counselor: So many times I've seen that you're able to take a whole picture of a situation and understand it, realizing other people's perspectives, and you know so many others don't do that. I have a feeling that *this strength may get the best of you sometimes and keep you from opening up to other people.*

Client: Yeah.

Counselor: So you protect yourself from people who can't do that, so that you're not disappointed?

Client: Yes.

Counselor: *What other strengths might you wish to tap into instead during these times?*

Client: I don't know. [pause] I'm able to look into myself to see what I need.

Counselor: You have insight not only about others but yourself as well?

Client: Yeah.

Counselor: *How can you tap into that?*

Client: I guess, I do know how to get out of a relationship that isn't good for me, so maybe I should focus on finding relationships with people who can be there for me.

Realizing that his separating himself from some people in his life may have developed partially out of his strength of being able to see different perspectives allows the client to understand the limitations of this strength. The client is able to recognize additional strengths he has for overcoming this struggle.

The discovery of strengths is not limited to this phase of counseling. Once counselors and clients become normalized to the essential force that strength recognition has on personal and familial change, not only will strengths recognized early in counseling continue to develop, but untapped resources and strengths will also emerge. This can occur during the second phase (Contracted Change) or the third phase (Developed Lifestyle). Remaining open to how the recognition and deliberate application of strengths begets the discovery and application of new strengths is a cycle of change that is both self-fulfilling and life enriching. As clients become aware of their strengths, strength-centered counselors help them also recognize how exclusive use of these strengths may prevent them from moving forward in resolving their struggles.

STEP 5: HOPE PERCEPTION

> *The longest journey of any person is the journey inward.*
>
> –Dag Hammarskjöld

Individuals seek counseling with hopes for change in the midst of dynamics that provide compelling reasons for not changing. There are times in most of our lives when the decision to make a life change (e.g., habit, relationship, career) is balanced with deciding not to make a life change (e.g., security, stability, consistency). This struggle can be further complicated when individuals anticipate that once certain conditions or symptoms are reduced, change will be easier:

"Once I lose weight, it will be easier to meet new people."

"Once the children are older, I will have more time to exercise."

"Once he [she] stops drinking, our relationship will be like it was."

"Once I stop feeling depressed, I will be happier."

"Once I can begin sleeping better, I will have more energy to get things done."

"Once I get more things done . . ."

This perspective can give the impression that change either happens or does not happen and can quickly lead to personal demoralization and a feeling of hopelessness when facing of life's challenges. This is in contrast to the change process introduced by Prochaska, DiClemente, and Norcross (1992). They contended that change was a spiralling continuum of five stages ranging from precontemplation to maintenance (see Figure 6.1).

Figure 6.1	Change Process

Rather than being a static event, change becomes a dynamic process defined by an increasing motivational readiness to progress through and between the stages of change. This is the essence of hope: a belief in and "readiness" for change prior to change occurring. Prochaska (2000) found that individuals who moved from one stage to the next doubled their chances for change and solving their presenting problem. Counseling is effective, therefore, because it reverses the demoralization that a black-or-white view of change can instill and restores hope that life will improve . . . and that appreciating the process of change is far more therapeutic than what the change might be. This is often counterintuitive to a perspective that contends that hopefulness/optimism occurs only after the symptoms are reduced (Frank & Frank, 1993), and requires counselors to have faith in the often imperceptible resources of clients as well as a trust in the counseling process and the emergent quality of therapeutic outcomes.

The following questions are intended to set the stage for this "leap of faith" required to progress through the stages of change necessary for developing a learned optimism (see Table 6.7). The first column of strategic questions overviews a general sequence in a conversation of hope with others, while the second seeks to use the image of a hope chest to provide clarity to the change process. It represents a more sequential experience for eliciting hope statements from others.

Table 6.7	Eliciting Hope	

Eliciting Hope "General Hope Sequence"	Eliciting Hope "Hope Chest"
"Tell me about a time you felt *hopeful* about your life and circumstances. What was going on in your life that made you feel hopeful?" "At that time, what *parts of yourself* did you have faith in? How might this have contributed to feeling more hopeful?" "When you felt more hopeful, how did you *remind* yourself to keep moving forward during difficult situations?"	"Let's suppose you could create a hope chest that would permit all your problems to go away. You can ask for three wishes from the hope chest. Although the three hopes will be granted, you must make changes to ensure their continuation." • "What three hopes would you take out of your hope chest?" • "How would the granting of these hopes change your present situation?" • "What would you have to do to keep your hopes alive?" • "What strengths do you have as a person to sustain your three hopes?"

Resilience

People who have been victimized do not need to relive or recount the pain as much as they need to have fostered a sense that they have survived in the face of adversity.

–Michael Clark (1997)

Clients and families are influencing their lives all the time, even in the most dismal circumstances. It is not that they are depressed, but how they have been able to keep depression at bay. It is not that they are worried, but how they have been able to keep worry from overtaking their lives. Depression and worry are simply by-products of the pursuit of a better life, the hope for something more and different, and the efforts reflected in every struggle. As important as understanding the perception that clients and families have in relationship to their problems and their struggle for change, highlighting the unique personal qualities and strengths marshaled against these problems is the intent of this phase of strength-centered counseling and central when separating "who I am" from "what I wish to change." Saleebey (1992) captured this perspective nicely in writing:

> At the very least, the strengths perspective obligates workers to understand that, however downtrodden or sick, individuals have survived (and in some cases even thrived). They have taken steps, summoned up resources, and coped. We need to know what they have done, how they have done it, what they have learned from doing it, what resources (inner and outer) were available in their struggle to surmount their troubles. People are always working on their situations, even if just deciding to be resigned to them; as helpers we must tap into that work, elucidate it, find and build on its possibilities. (pp. 171–172)

Wagnild and Young (1990) defined resiliency as the ability to restore balance following a difficult experience and integrate it into the backdrop of one's total life experiences. This emphasis on the struggle "through adversity" is also highlighted by Rak and Patterson (1996), who went on to explain that resiliency was people's ability to progress in their development despite being "bent," "compressed," or "stretched" by factors in often risky environments. It is the innate capacity of individuals to bounce back from failure, setbacks, and disappointments (Desetta & Wolin, 2000).

Attributes associated with "buffering" these life difficulties appear to be active problem solving, the capacity to gain positive attention from others, optimism, high self-regard, and having a proactive perspective toward life (Bogar & Hulse-Killacky, 2006). Individuals' recognition of their own strengths in the face of life's struggles provides hope as well as a route to authentic self-esteem. A strength-centered counseling relationship, therefore, seeks to restore clients' belief in themselves and the control they have over events in their lives. It is to assess and understand people on their strengths rather than solely on their problems.

Prior to establishing goals, the questions in Table 6.8 provide a concluding dialogue of the resilient patterns that individuals and families use to stand up to the adverse influence of their problems. It is a final shift away from personal deficit focus and an intentional clinical effort toward recognizing qualities of personal, social, and cultural resilience.

Table 6.8 Resilience Questions	

"This has been very difficult for you. How have you *managed* to keep things from getting worse?"

"You found the energy and time to see me today. How have you *managed* to keep your sanity and hope in the midst of these problems? What is your guess about how you developed these strengths?"

"What qualities do you *possess* that you seem to be able to tap into in times of adversity? What would *others* say are the qualities that you have that keep you going?"

"What aspects of your heritage sustain you in times of difficulty? Who in your life was your "cultural coach," and what does he or she whisper in your ear? How is this useful to you?"

Counselor:	This has been very difficult for you. How have you managed to keep things from getting worse?
Client:	They can hardly get any worse (weeping).
Counselor:	You're here. You made it in to see me today. How did you find the energy to get here today? You had to go through some trouble to get here, too—getting someone to bring you. You're going to your job from here. How do you manage to keep going? To keep things from getting worse?
Client:	You know, I buy them things. Even though I can't see them anymore, I keep a box of things that I would give to them if I could. If I'm out and I see a toy or a small stuffed animal I get it.
Counselor:	Those presents keep you hopeful that your kids will know that you do love them.
Client:	Yes. I do love them (straightens up and wipes her eyes). I do love them, and I know they have good parents now. Maybe I will get to see them when they're older, and then I can give them these things.
Counselor:	You manage to *keep your sanity* by keeping the connection between you and your kids around you with those presents. Is that it?
Client:	Yes.
Counselor:	You believe in being a good mom. You believe a mom should take care of her kids, and you knew you couldn't do that for them right now.
Client:	Yes—I do believe in being a good mom, and I know a good mom should take care of her kids. I'm trying to get my life together, but I'm not going to try and get them back. That's not fair to them, but I do hope when they're older they'll know who I am.
Counselor:	You want them to know that you believe in being a good mom, and that you wanted them to have a good mom too.
Client:	Yes. It's so hard to know they have a good mom, and it's not me.
Counselor:	You also believe in doing what you think is right even when it's hard. What other qualities do you *possess* that you seem to be able to tap into in times like these?
Client:	I'm still here. Somehow I'm still here. I want them to know that even though I'm not taking care of them now, I want to. I wish I could. I know they have a nice place to live now. I really do keep trying.
Counselor:	You're a hard worker.
Client:	I am. Maybe they'll have that too.

There is a fable about the sun and wind having a dispute as to who was the most powerful. They saw a man walking along and they challenged each other about which of them would be most successful at getting the man to remove his coat. The wind started first and blew up a huge gale, the coat flapped but the man only closed all his buttons and tightened up his belt. The sun tried next and shone brightly, making the man sweat. He proceeded to take off his coat (Bryant, 2008). Counseling that emanates as a wind often encounters self-protective strategies as clients guard against the chill of change. In this initial phase of strength-centered counseling (*shared understanding*), practitioners are encouraged to be more like the sun. The use of warmth and comfort provides an atmosphere where clients and families are invited to unveil hidden strengths and resources in anticipation of difficulties the wind might bring.

Assisting clients and families with understanding their struggles through a context of strengths and possibilities, rather than personal deficits and problems, instills a hope for change. It also establishes engaged understanding between counselors and clients needed to progress effectively through the phases of strength-centered counseling and allows clients an opportunity to shed their coats so as to feel the warmth of the sun and the self-healing tendencies this can provoke.

PROFESSIONAL GROWTH ACTIVITY: STRENGTHS FROM PROBLEMS

Change with a learning partner between roles where the "client" briefly shares a recent problem and the "counselor" looks for opportunities to reflect back only the following:

- What the problem implies about the personal values being challenged by the problem as well as implied preferences for the person's life/relationship
- What the client has *learned about himself or herself* in attempting to keep things from getting worse
- The personal *strengths* apparent in the face of the problem (adversity)

Discuss your reactions with one another on how this might be different from other avenues of exploring client and family struggles.

PROFESSIONAL GROWTH ACTIVITY: STRENGTH-FOCUSED ROLE-PLAY

In triads, rotate among the following roles:

Client

- Revisit current life struggle or difficulty

Counselor

- Elicit and reflect back inherent and implied strengths (see Table 5.1, Strength Characteristics, in Chapter 5) or utilize Strength Reflections (see Table 4.2, Chapter 4) to elicit strengths directly.

Observer

- Provide feedback about counselor's strengths and windows of opportunity (e.g., strengths, acceptance, ambivalence).

PROFESSIONAL GROWTH ACTIVITY: THE VIA

Part 1

Please visit the VIA Web site to register and take the strength inventory: http://www.via survey.org/Account/Register/

Upon your review, please select two or three strengths and apply them deliberately throughout the week. Pay attention to the effect this has on you as well as those around you. Also, reflect on those moments when your strengths, despite your best efforts, get the best of you. Examples of these dichotomies are below:

Strength: Curiosity and interest in the world. You are curious about everything. You are always asking question, and you find all subjects and topics fascinating. You like exploration and discovery

Value: Knowledge

Dichotomy: This may get in the way when asking too many questions/gathering too much information, leading to a lack of focus or inability to get to decision making.

Strength: Judgment, critical thinking and open-mindedness. Thinking things through and examining them from all sides are important aspects of who you are. You do not jump to conclusions, and you rely on only solid evidence to make your decisions. You are able to change your mind.

Value: Thoughtful decision making

Dichotomy: This may cause frustration when information is unavailable.

Strength: Capacity to love and be loved. You value close relations with others, in particular those in which sharing and caring are reciprocated. The people to whom you feel most close are the same people who feel most close to you.

Value: Responsible relationships

Dichotomy: This may cause frustration and dissatisfaction when interacting in unbalanced relationships.

Part 2

Pay attention to your interactions during the week and *make note* of how you might apply a strength perspective. How might this shift the conversation?

COUNSELOR INTERVIEW & REFLECTION GUIDE

Shared Understanding: The Steps[a]

Focus	Intervention
Step 1: Problem Perception	Problem Perception "So, how were you hoping I could help you?" "Can you think of a name to call this problem? What is it like (picture/metaphor)?" "Are there other problems that this teams up with? In what ways does it do this?" Problem Impact "What impact has the problem had on you/others?" "How has the problem robbed you of what you want?" "How does the problem 'get the best of you'? What has it promised you?" "What do you think will happen if you do not make a change?" Problem Influence "What does the problem whisper in your ear?" "Would the problem want you in counseling? How did it try to keep you from coming?" "How much of your life does it control? Is this your preferred way of being or would you prefer something else?" "Who else might be an advocate for you in standing up to the influence of the problem?" Exploring Explanations "What is your theory about why change has been difficult for you?" "How have you tried to solve this, and why have those efforts proven unsuccessful until now?" "So, the problem is _____ and what you want is _____." Identifying Expectations "When things are more on track, what will be different in you as well as in your life?" "How will you know when counseling is no longer necessary?" Eliciting a Change Conversation "In what ways would it be good for you to change or 'do something different'?" "If you did decide to change, how would you do it? What would be your reasons for doing something different?" "What are the good things about change and what are the not so good things?"

Focus	Intervention
Step 2: Struggle Perception	Strengths Within the Struggle "With all that you are managing right now, it makes complete sense you are tired and depressed. Your fatigue is likely more about the load you are carrying than about you. In fact, I am a bit surprised that things haven't become worse. How have you *managed* to keep your head above water?" "Talk about those qualities you have *learned* about yourself that assist in sustaining yourself in the face of stress. What would *others* say about the qualities that you have that keep you going during these periods?" "What *advice* do you give to yourself that helps you keep your head above water and reminds you to keep moving forward?" "When was the last time you felt *hopeful* about your life and circumstances? What was going on in your life that made you feel hopeful?"
Step 3: Strength Perception	Eliciting General Strengths "What are the best things about you? What is your guess about how they were developed?" "What special characteristics or talents distinguish you from others?" "What do you wish others might discover about you?" "When are your strengths most useful for you? When are they not? What is your theory about this?" Anchoring Strengths "How might some of these attitudes, beliefs, and strengths be adapted and applied to your current difficulties?" "What strengths do you believe you need to develop to better address the difficulties we have discussed?" "How have you managed to keep things from getting worse?" Additional Strength Questions "What do you do well?" "What do other people look to you for?" "What are your outstanding qualities?" "How and with whom do you build alliances?" "How have you been able to adapt to change?" "Tell me what you do when you are at your best."
Step 4: Dichotomy Perception	Dichotomy of Strengths Summary of Strengths (see previous steps) "Discuss how, despite your best intentions, these qualities/strengths get the best of you at times. How is this true in your current struggles? What other strengths might you wish to tap into instead during these times?"

(Continued)

(Continued)

Focus	Intervention
Step 5: Hope Perception	General Hope Sequence "Tell me about a time you felt *hopeful* about your life and circumstances? What was going on in your life that made you feel hopeful?" "At that time, what *parts of yourself* did you have faith in? How might this have contributed to feeling more hopeful?" "When you felt more hopeful, how did you *remind* yourself to keep moving forward during difficult times?" Hope Chest "Let's suppose you could create a hope chest that would permit all your problems to go away. You can make a request to take out of the hope chest three wishes. Although the three hopes will be granted, you must make changes to ensure their continuation." "What three hopes would you take out of your hope chest?" "How would the granting of these hopes change your present situation?" "What would you have to do to keep your hopes alive? "What strengths do you have as a person to sustain your three hopes?" Patterns of Resilience "This has been very difficult for you. How have you *managed* to keep things from getting worse?" "You found the energy and time to see me today. How have you *managed* to keep your sanity and hope in the midst of these problems? What is your guess about how you developed these?" "What qualities do you *possess* that you seem to be able to tap into in times of adversity? What would *others* say are the qualities that you have that keep you going?" "What aspects of your heritage sustain you in times of difficulty? Who in your life was your 'cultural coach' and what does he or she whisper in your ear? How is this useful to you?"

Note: a. When limited by time, a recommended abbreviated sequence is (a) Problem Impact, (b) Strengths Within the Struggle, (c) Dichotomy of Strengths, and (d) Patterns of Resilience.

Phase 2: Contracted Change

Envisioning a Preferred Life

    Perception of the Preferences

    Solution Efforts

    The Miracle, the Dream, and the Future

    The Road Ahead

    Building a Readiness

Understanding Goals

    Scaling Steps of Action

    Follow-Up Suggestions

    The Theory of Holes

Strength-Centeredness Model: Contracted Change

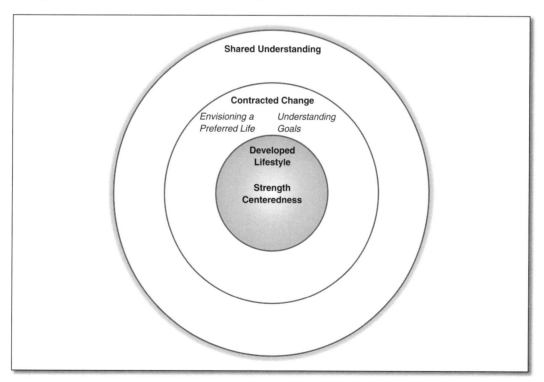

Envisioning a Preferred Life

We also believe that when we think we know what our client's experience is, we are probably cutting ourselves off from the client and from further possibilities of experience.

–Walter & Peller (1996)

Individuals seeking counseling do so with hope for change. Every helping encounter is an implied contract and centers less on "why" a problem or set of problems exists and more on "what" can be different and "how" these differences might happen. This underlying current of hope is often presented in stories of hopelessness and can be overlooked by well-meaning counselors assisting individuals with a "retelling" of their stories. If this is all that occurs, people can leave such interviews feeling drained by the experience—having only reinforced conclusions of hopelessness and exhaustion in facing life circumstances. Eventually, this fatigue can become a reminder of personal weakness and deficits rather than being about the problems themselves. The hope for change becomes buried beneath the daily weight of worry and despair. A problem-focused clinical conversation clouds over the rays of hope in each story of hopelessness, and ignores the available strengths and resources individuals possess for standing up to daily distress. As Clark (1997) pointed out, it is far more therapeutic to foster the fact that people have survived in the face of adversity than to relive or recount the pain they have been living with.

A hope for change is also a contract for something "preferred" in light of something that is not. Often the goals are formally or informally agreed upon with individuals defining change from the negative with a focus on merely the "absence" of a problem or set of symptoms. Change is more than just becoming "less" depressed, angry, anxious, stressed, inappropriate, and/or hopeless. From a strength-centered perspective, the goals of counseling are stated in the positive tense and directed toward future changes. In collaboration with clients, counselors establish goals that sustain people with the courage, optimism, personal responsibility, interpersonal skills, perseverance, and purpose needed to overcome adversity. The emotional fatigue often experienced in life's most complicated problems is about the climb and not the climber, and counseling rests on the inherent strengths and resources that people have from overcoming their concerns. Strength-centered counseling addresses the problem, and not just personal deficits or perceived deficiencies.

Another aspect of the phrase "the exhaustion is due to what the person's carrying around, not the person" is helping me to see individuals separate from their problem. It is also helping me to gain a stronger hold on their preferences. When the problem is center stage, nothing else can be seen but that. With the language of strength-centered counseling, the problem can be moved to the side, allowing the helper and helpee to both look at the problem and discuss it from a more equal footing. The helpee can self-reflect from a clearer view, more free from the values of the issues. –Lindsay W.

By separating clients from the weight of their problems, strength-centered counselors elicit a conversation of hope through appreciating struggles, and understanding that for every expressed problem there is an implied preference for something different. In this phase, Contracted Change, we introduce strategies for identifying goals beneath the surface of personal and life struggles. In addition, we offer examples of questions that assist with painting a picture of a preferred life. Finally, we guide you in assessing a client's level of readiness and motivation in moving, in even in small steps, toward his or her preferred way of being and living.

PERCEPTION OF PREFERENCES

We may think there is willpower involved, but more likely . . . change is due to want power. Wanting the new addiction more than the old one. Wanting the new me in preference to the person I am now.

–George Sheehan

In this phase of strength-centered counseling, rekindling hope from stories of frustration and hopelessness is paramount. For each problem there is an anticipated solution. As long as the dialogue of counseling remains on the problem, the experience of the solution will be mired in overcoming personal deficits or social shortcomings. It will be as if the client and counselor are seeking to find the missing piece of a puzzle. As long as the piece remains undiscovered, the feelings of helplessness and hopelessness will also remain. G. Miller and de Shazer (1998) indicated that problems may actually be unconnected or "irrelevant to the change process" (p. 370), while De Jong and Berg (1998) argued that solutions are *constructed* between the client and counselor rather than *occurring* merely through solving problems together. A strength-centered perspective seeks to understand not only how life difficulties and problems impact and influence people, but also how they reflect the hopes and preferences people have for their lives.

From a strength-centered perspective, every problem implies a preferred outcome. The experience of anxiety implies a wish for peace and acceptance; the experience of depression implies a hope for happiness and joy; and the experience of conflict and frustration implies a goal of harmony and belonging. Table 7.1 offers examples of how most problem statements imply a wish for a preferred future. They represent listening responses intended to highlight the inherent struggle between the problem and the solution. As O'Hanlon (2003)

Table 7.1	Problem Statements and Implied Preferences

A Client Problem Statement	A Counselor Preference Reflection
"Nobody likes me at school and I don't have any close friends."	"Sounds like you would like to have friends who know you a bit better and who have a different perception of you. Is that it?"
"She won't follow the rules in our house, and no matter how hard I have tried, we just end up fighting."	"You would wish her to know how much you care for her and wish her to be responsible and safe. Is that it?"
	"You would prefer to communicate with your daughter in ways more consistent with the care you feel toward her. Do I have that right?"
"I have tried quitting smoking, but I keep slipping back. I don't know what else to do."	"So, you see the importance and challenges of abstinence and you are hoping we might be able to find ways to tackle this thing. Is that it?"

pointed out in his review of inclusive listening skills, the "problem has occurred . . . in the future things can be different" (p. 88).

> So the question for me was "How do I incorporate my strength-centered belief system in working with batterers?" One of the members informed us that it was the final week in his 26-week ordered attendance. I asked if he could share with the group his plans for continuing his growth after leaving the group (identifying the strength he possesses to continue his work). He discussed the changes he had experienced in his thought process since attending the batterer's group and that he would continue seeing an individual counselor to work on his depression and anger.
>
> "I want to thank you for your participation in this group. You have shown great courage in opening yourself up and sharing very difficult information. It speaks to your commitment to becoming a better man, father, and husband that you plan to continue your counseling. You have what it takes to continue healing." He began to cry. He said that no one had thanked him or acknowledged how difficult this process had been for him. "It means a lot to me that you said that." The other group members nodded, clearly impacted by the moment.
>
> How do we help individuals who are court-ordered for counseling to see it as an opportunity rather than a punishment? Strength-centered counseling has taught me that it is not by praising them for their attendance, as that is merely a pat on the back. Rather, we need to help them see the strength, courage, and commitment to self that is evidenced through their continued attendance and disclosure. Strength-centered counseling not only tells clients that we see them and their strengths clearly, but helps them find the strengths they didn't even know they had. –Michelle B.

Listening for preferences in statements of frustration, anger, and despair is a central skill for strength-centered counselors during this phase of counseling. Balancing a shared understanding of the concerns that people express with an appreciation of the implied preferences in relation to those concerns highlights the healing properties inherent in a multi-dimensional view. For clients and families, this demonstrates the recognition of overwhelming difficulties with a simultaneous perspective of the inherent preferences they have for themselves, their family, and their lives. For many, a better life has little to do with the absence of a struggle, but rather an understanding and willingness not to let the struggle "get the best of them." It is looking at change from the vantage point of "and/both" rather than "either/or." It is a fundamental aspect of postmodernism and an essential process of strength-centered counseling when developing a direction clients wish for themselves. The experiential activity below is designed to assist with appreciating this important clinical dynamic in strength-centered counseling. With a learning partner, rotate between roles and reflect on your experiences with one another as well as how this might differ from other personal or professional exchanges.

Activity: Preferences From Problems

Person A (Client)

Express a current life difficulty.

Person B (Strength-Centered Counselor)

Listen and respond empathically to the difficulty. When ready, provide a reflection that articulates:

a. The problem and the client's experience with the problem

b. What the problem implies about future preferences

c. Personal strengths apparent in the client's struggle for "something different"

Change roles and reflect on the experience.

SOLUTION EFFORTS

The eye sees only what the mind is prepared to comprehend.

–Henri Bergson

In addition to reflecting preferences in the face of life problems, strength-centered counselors seek to directly elicit past solution efforts. Individuals struggling with problems often discount mild exceptions when problems do not occur or are less "problematic." Burns, a cognitive theorist, articulated in 1989 that it is common to begin to see life as a never-ending series of negative events. When governed by strong emotions, the mind becomes a filter, letting into awareness only those thoughts that reinforce that mood. In other words, the more a client reexperiences the negative moods associated with the problems presented in counseling, the more unlikely change will seem. Because people rarely stop to question this cycle, directly exploring those times when problems are absent or having less influence can be highly useful in understanding the preferences that individuals and families have in light of their problems and life struggles.

The questions in Table 7.2 elicit *solution efforts* that highlight unseen strengths and introduce the idea that problems are not always occurring (exceptions) and provide a window into future "ways of being" (unique outcomes). They further guide well-meaning counselors away from the temptation to judge or blame clients for their difficulties and encourage a mutual discovery of how clients have managed to experience moments when life appears "more preferable."

Even in the bleakest circumstances, resources, strengths, and exceptions to the problem pattern can be gleaned through a conversation about daily events where the smallest details can contradict perceptions of defeat and hopelessness. The following activity is designed

Table 7.2 Solution Efforts

Solution Efforts: Exceptions	Solution Efforts: Unique Outcomes
"When would you say the problem has less influence on you? How do you explain this?" "What is different about you during those times when the problem doesn't occur or has less influence? What are you doing differently? What advice are you giving yourself? What is happening differently around you?" "What do you do so that you don't have this problem then? Where did you get the idea to do it differently at those times? Whose idea was it to do it that way?" "Do you think this (problem/struggle) should speak for you or do you think it would be better for you to speak for yourself? How will others know that this decision is becoming clearer for you?" (Adapted from de Shazer, 1988)	"What do you do to keep the problem at bay when you need to? How were you able to weaken the influence of the problem?" "When does the problem have less influence on you? What is your guess about why?" "Has there ever been a time when the problem might have occurred but didn't?" "How were you able to do that then? What was different about you at that time?" "Who is in your corner helping with your efforts to reduce the influence the problem has on you and those around you? What advice might they provide?" (Adapted from White & Epston, 1990)

to encourage a measure of hope and readiness for future change by focusing on those experiences where problems have less influence on people's lives. Working with a learning partner, complete the activity below.

Activity: Solution Efforts

Person A (Client)

Express a current life difficulty.

Person B (Strength-Centered Counselor)

Listen and respond empathically to the difficulty and utilize one of the Solution Effort questions in Table 7.2.

Respond empathically to the initial solution effort response, and follow up with, *"What else is different?"*

Trade roles and reflect on the experience.

THE MIRACLE, THE DREAM, AND THE FUTURE

Some men see things as they are and say why . . . I dream of things that never were and say why not.

–George Bernard Shaw

The ability to visualize change increases the probability that the change will occur. Setting goals that visualize a positive outcome has the tendency to focus the client's energies and hope for success (Cormier & Cormier, 1998). People are motivated to change dysfunctional or self-defeating behaviors because they hope that doing so will effect the desired life changes and bring anticipated rewards, indicating their "preferred life." When an individual paints a picture of this future detailing the steps, thoughts, and interactions likely to occur as the change emerges, hope for this change also occurs.

Milton Erickson (1954) introduced this as working backward from the end-goal and utilized the "pseudo-orientation in time" technique. Clients were asked to imagine looking into a crystal ball and to describe how they were able to solve their problems upon meeting their therapist at some time in the future. Steve de Shazer (1985) paralleled this idea through the use of a "miracle question" that encouraged clients to imagine a life when the problem was solved and "more on track." Each emphasized an inductive shift with clients. Rather than formulating a treatment plan deduced from reported symptoms, diagnostic clarity, and a review of life problems, they sought solution descriptions generated from clients. To better experience this shift in both perspective and descriptive language, attempt the activity below and reflect on your reactions with a learning partner.

Activity: Imagining Change

Step 1

- Get comfortable in a chair and take a few breaths, with a brief pause after each one.
- Focus your concentration on imagining the chair you are in is not there . . . focus intently on this.

Step 2

- Now, imagine that the chair you currently sit in is made of a fine, luxurious, richly textured, and amazingly comfortable leather. The most relaxing and comfortable chair you have ever sat in . . . focus intently on this.

Step 3

- With a learning partner, discuss which was easier to do.

How might this experience be related to goal formation with others?

What you may have discovered with the activity above is that it is often far easier to imagine the inclusion of a preferred life rather than just the absence of one that is not. This intent assumes that the future "is not a slave of the past events in a person's life; therefore, in spite of past traumatic events, a person can negotiate and implement many useful steps that are likely to lead him/her to a more satisfying life" (Berg & Dolan, 2001, p. 4). Therefore, the following questions aim at promoting a process with clients that shifts them away from the "known past" toward a "preferred life." Resources, skills, and advice can be unveiled through the use of one of the sequences of questions in Table 7.3. Additional questions are presented to assist with anchoring the elements of a preferred life with the strengths and resources available to clients.

It is important to note that these questions are an initial step in conceptualizing with clients and families a life beyond, or in spite of, life struggles. The work of these strategic questions lies not only in *what* the miracle, dream, and/or future life might be, but also with *how* the miracle, dream, and/or future life occur. Asking any of these questions enables clients to begin exploring the life they would like to have. They begin to envision the preferences they desire. Grounded in the belief that people harbor the strengths and potential self-directed change, strength-centered counselors provide a tenacious presence to assist with eliciting those actions, thoughts, and interactions contributing to preferred ways of being. It is a mutual discovery of (a) how clients will stand up to adversity and address life problems, (b) ways in which their personal qualities will be applied toward solutions, and (c) who will notice the initial signs that change is beginning to occur. The transcript below highlights the use of a preferred life question as well as efforts to elicit clarity in the change process.

| Table 7.3 | Miracle, Dream, and Future Questions | |

Miracle Question[a] (Broad-Based Solution-Focused Inquiry)	Follow-Up Questions
"*Suppose* that when you go to sleep tonight, a miracle occurs, and because you were sleeping, you didn't know it happened. The miracle solved the problem that brought you here. When you wake up in the morning, what clues will you see that lead you to discover that this miracle has taken place?" [Adults]	"What else would be different?" "What would you notice in the advice you give yourself?" "Who would be the first to notice that something had changed?"
"If I had a magic wand and could wave it over your head and the problem that brought you here disappeared, what would be different and what would you like to see yourself doing?" [Children]	"What else would be different?" "Who would be the first to notice you're doing something different?"
The Dream Question[b] (Intrinsic-Based Solution-Focused Inquiry)	Follow-Up Questions
"*Suppose* that tonight while you are sleeping you have a dream. In this dream you discover the answers and resources you need to solve the problem that you are concerned about right now. When you wake up tomorrow, you may or may not remember your dream; however, you do notice that you are different. As you go about your day, how will you know that you discovered or developed the skills and resources necessary to solve your problem?"	"What else would be different?" "What will be the first small bit of evidence that you did this?" "Who will be the first to notice, and what will that person see different in you?"
Future Question (Concrete-Based Solution-Focused Inquiry)	Follow-Up Question
"*Imagine* yourself in the future when the problem is no longer a problem. Tell me where you are, what you are doing and saying, and what others around you are doing and saying."	"What else would be different?"

Sources: a. Adapted from De Jong & Berg (2002).

    b. Adapted from Greene, Lee, Mentzer, Pinnell, & Niles (1998).

Counselor: So you're at a point in your life where you're letting go of something that has been a big part of your life, and you're moving into something different, but you have a lot of uncertainty. Is that it?

Client: Um-hum. Yeah, it's a little scary.

Counselor: A little scary.

Client: I've never had another job. I mean I've had different positions, but I've been with this company for the past 40 years.

Counselor: *Suppose that when you go to sleep tonight, a miracle occurs, and because you were sleeping, you didn't know it happened. The miracle solved the problem that brought you here. When you wake up in the morning, what clues will you see that lead you to discover that this miracle has taken place?*

Client: Well, I guess I'd wake up and know what I was going to do that day.

Counselor: OK, *what else?*

Client: I guess that would get rid of the feeling that I didn't know what I was going to do that day.

Counselor: You'd be more resolved?

Client: I'd feel less unsure.

Counselor: Less unsure, and more of what?

Client: Content. Content, even though I didn't know what was going to happen. I guess, I'd get up and get dressed to go to work, if I'd made that decision, or I'd get dressed and go to school, if I'd made that decision. In any case, I'd have the feeling I was OK.

Counselor: That you were OK. *Who would be the first to know there was a change?*

Client: Probably my husband.

Counselor: And what would that look like?

Client: He probably wouldn't be tip-toeing around trying not to ask me the wrong questions, so our conversation would feel a bit easier.

Counselor: *Tell me about that. What would be different during your conversation?*

Client: Maybe I'd be able to ask him something about him, and he'd actually answer.

Counselor: Maybe you'd show an interest in his life?

Client: Instead of always talking about how I'm feeling in an artificial way. More of a normal exchange.

Counselor: Would you like that?

Client: Yeah, yeah, I would.

Counselor: Tell me more about that—*what else you would like more of?*

Client: The feeling that I could talk about what was bothering me without a cheerful smile like everything was going to be OK. That I wouldn't feel embarrassed.

Counselor: *What would you feel instead?*

Client: Really OK that I got fired.

In this case, answering the Miracle Question allowed the client the opportunity to begin identifying what she would like to see going on in her life and how she would be acting in response to others in her surroundings. She begins envisioning her preferred life.

Frankl (1963) concluded that having a feeling of purpose in one's life can alleviate distress and buffer life's disappointments. Similarly, a strength-centered counselor establishes a relationship and dialogue that encourage clients to find meaning through envisioning a preferred life in the face of adverse circumstances. The therapeutic intent of Miracle, Dream, and Future questions is to assist individuals with articulating and expanding on solutions they hope for themselves. In the same way that trips are first planned by deciding on a destination, envisioning one's preferred life can serve as a guide to the road ahead. This is not only central for establishing a different set of options for defining and responding to problems, but it also begins to outline *contracted change* that individuals and families formulate with counselors.

THE ROAD AHEAD

It's a mistake to look for an explanation when all you need is a description of how things work.

—Ludwig Wittgenstein

To encourage articulating the detail needed to assist clients and families in navigating the road ahead once the elements of a preferred life are identified, "Video Talk" and "Mind-Mapping" can be useful. The sequence of these questions can assist clients with better understanding the initial steps and benchmarks necessary for seeing a preferred life take shape (see Table 7.4). The questions are intended to articulate the thoughts, beliefs, values, and resources specific to the goals for change. Furthermore, these questions can increase an individual's confidence that reaching the destination is not only possible, but likely.

As you will notice in the counselor–client dialogue below, the questions are strictly tools of the empathic skills of the counselor and his or her commitment to the descriptive process of bringing color and clarity to proposed visions of change by clients.

| **Table 7.4** | Video Talk and Mind Mapping | |

Video Talk	Mind Mapping
"If I were to *watch* you during the time when a miracle was occurring, what behaviors would I see you doing differently?"	"What is your theory about how you were able to do that as you think about the miracle/future? How do you account for these changes?"
"What *advice* would you be giving yourself (cognitions)?"	"What advice will you be giving yourself when the changes you are talking about begin to occur, even just a bit?"
"What *would* we see you feeling (emotion)?"	"How will you be able to stay on track in spite of all the distractions?

Client:	This has been going on for years. Sometimes it's not as bad, when I haven't been home in a while. Then we're all glad to see each other, so everyone is pleasant.
Counselor:	How are these times when the problem is a bit better different from other times?
Client:	I feel happier; I'm enjoying myself more. I'm not already feeling like it's time to go already.
Counselor:	You feel like it's nice to be there. *If I were to* watch *you during the time when this was occurring, what behaviors would I see you doing differently?*
Client:	I guess (laughs) I wouldn't be rolling my eyes.
Counselor:	OK, eyes would be still (laughs). *What else would the videotape capture?*
Client:	I'd probably be in conversation more with my mother [rather] than just "lecturing" her about what she should be doing.
Counselor:	You'd prefer that, being in conversation with your mom? You'd enjoy that?
Client:	It would be nicer. It would feel comfortable, without waiting for an argument to start.
Counselor:	*What advice would you be giving yourself (cognitions)?* To keep this atmosphere?
Client:	I guess I'd be warning myself not to talk too much. Not to get worked up. I tend to get upset when my mother mentions anything to me about something not being just right, and I start focusing on everything she does that isn't just right.
Counselor:	So you'd advise yourself to watch what you say.
Client:	Yes. Then it might stay pleasant.
Counselor:	In the video, *what would we see you feeling (emotion)?*
Client:	I'd be smiling and at ease. I guess I'd feel relaxed, happy.

BUILDING A READINESS

A more productive and fascinating question, we believe, is why people do change, for change also is the norm. In time, people adjust to new lifestyles. . . . In spite of themselves, teenagers usually grow up. What is it that awakens us and causes a gradual course correction—or even a dramatic turnabout?

—W. R. Miller and Rollnick (2002)

Growing evidence suggests that tailoring treatment to the client's stage of readiness can improve the likelihood of successful counseling outcomes (Prochaska, 2007). Establishing goals beyond their level of motivation can overwhelm clients, engender resistance, and often cause them to continue a cycle of perceived failure and hopelessness. On the other hand, developing goals below a client's level of motivation can impact the level of trust a client has in the counselor to assist with overcoming problems, as shown in Figure 7.1.

Figure 7.1 Stages of Change

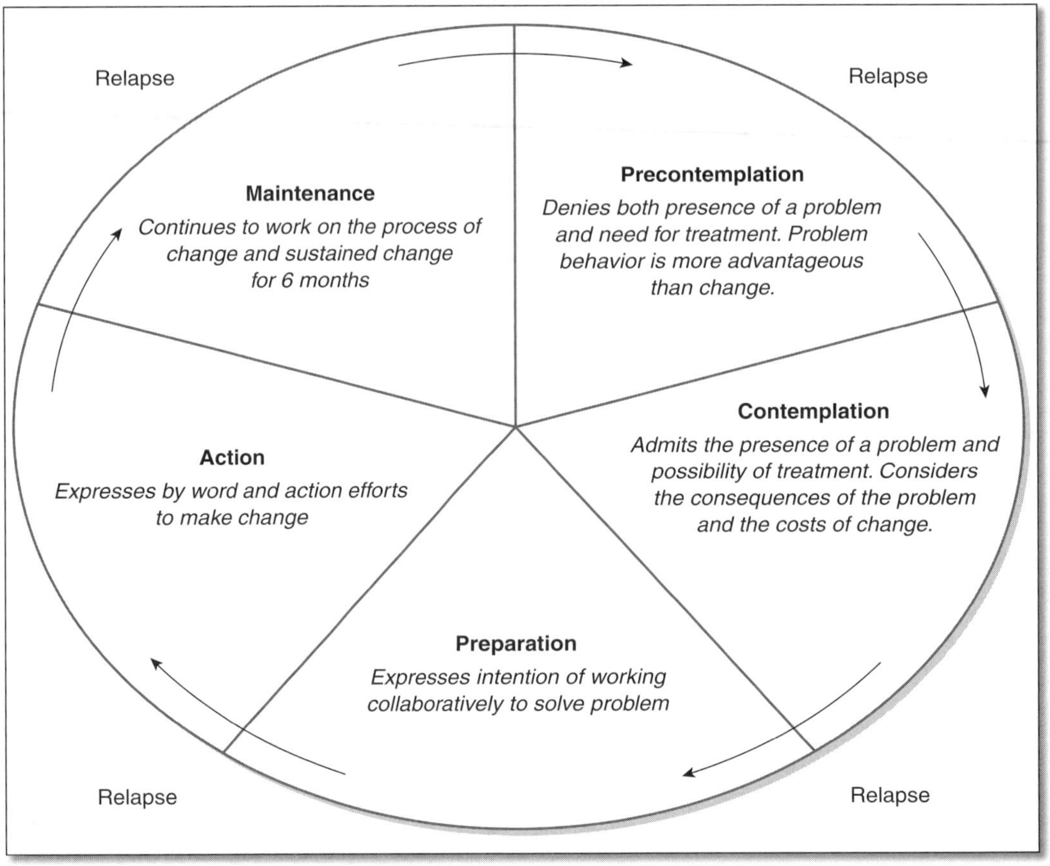

Relapse

Relapse

Maintenance
Continues to work on the process of change and sustained change for 6 months

Precontemplation
Denies both presence of a problem and need for treatment. Problem behavior is more advantageous than change.

Action
Expresses by word and action efforts to make change

Contemplation
Admits the presence of a problem and possibility of treatment. Considers the consequences of the problem and the costs of change.

Preparation
Expresses intention of working collaboratively to solve problem

Relapse

Relapse

Readiness questions elicit a conversation focused on strengths and a readiness for change in relationship to the goals of counseling (see Table 7.5). These readiness questions can help identify goals that are "just right" for a client's readiness to change. They also assist with increasing levels of motivation for moving from one stage of change to another.

Table 7.5	Readiness Questions	

Clinical Focus	Readiness Questions
Intention of Change	"What will you notice in yourself and those around you as you get more comfortable with 'idea' of the changes we talked about today?"
The Strengths of Change	"What is there about you, what strong points that we have discussed or that you know about yourself, that could help you succeed in making this change? Who else knows this and could help in this change?"
Hypothetical Change	"*Suppose* that you did succeed and are looking back at it now. What most likely is it that worked? How did it happen?" "What obstacles were you able to overcome and how?" "*Suppose* that this one big obstacle weren't there. If that obstacle were removed, then how might you go about making the change?" "*Clearly* you are feeling very discouraged about this. Use your imagination. If you were to try again, what might be the best way to try?"

Client:	I remember what you told me about how we can spiral up as much as we usually spiral down, so I stopped nagging on Saturday.
Counselor:	*What was there about you on Saturday, what did you have that day that helped you succeed in making this change?*
Client:	I don't know. I could just feel it coming. You know, same old thing. The house was a mess, it was Saturday morning, we'd both been busy all week, nothing was done, and we'd wanted to take the boys out for breakfast. I was so close to nagging about how could we go out when we had so much to take care of at home, and I just stopped myself.
Counselor:	So you were able to demonstrate some restraint, self-control?
Client:	Maybe, but it wasn't that much of a success. As soon as we got home, he went and watched the game and left the mess to me, so I had to say something, and well—you know.

Counselor:	What do you think was different about the time before you went out for breakfast?
Client:	I wanted to maintain the peace, and I guess I wanted to go out for breakfast. But then afterward we ended up arguing anyway. He didn't want to do chores, and I did not want to do them alone.
Counselor:	*Clearly you are feeling very discouraged about this. Use your imagination. If you were to try again, what might be the best way to try?*
Client:	I guess I wouldn't worry about what he was going to do, and concentrate on what I wanted to have happen.
Counselor:	*What makes you think that if you did decide to concentrate on what you would like to see happen, that you could do it? What encourages you that you can change if you want to?*
Client:	At work, I make decisions all the time. I have most of the rest of my life in order, so if I decide that I'm going to concentrate on what I want and not worry about what he wants, I know that I do that other places when it is the right thing to do, you know without neglecting my responsibilities.
Counselor:	(shows client the Readiness Ruler, included in "Professional Growth Activity: Readiness Ruler" below) *On a scale from 0 to 10, with 0 indicating that you are not ready to make a change and 10 indicating that you are completely ready, where would you place yourself on the Readiness Ruler for making a change toward solving your problem?*
Client:	I guess, I'm at about a three.
Counselor:	Ok, three. *How would you like to be able to rate your readiness for change?*
Client:	Nine—I know I want to do this.
Counselor:	*What would indicate to you that you are moving toward your desired rating?*
Client:	I wouldn't feel nervous saying what I would like to see happen, but then I wouldn't get upset, if he doesn't help it happen, and I would go ahead and do what I'd planned.

Contracted change involves counselors' intentional efforts to assist others with visualizing a preferred future rather than dwelling on past deficits. Because change occurs in stages, rather than in either/or events, strength-centered counselors take the necessary time to build a readiness as individuals contemplate and plan for a preferred life. Anchoring these preferred elements to the strengths and resources already present in clients imparts optimism and confidence. This hope for a better life or future sustains a client's positive participation or involvement in counseling and mobilizes the individual's efforts toward change (Snyder et al., 2000). This chapter provides the tools necessary to capture this hope with others and contract with them a future road that Scott Peck (1998) once described as the one "less traveled" to their preferred life.

Finally, *contracted change* with others embodies an understanding that people are always working to overcome life's challenges. The collaboration rests not with prescribing something new, but with discovering those strengths, resources, perspectives, and activities already present in people seeking "something different" in their lives. Saleebey (1992) captured this nicely when he wrote:

> At the very least, the strengths perspective obligates workers to understand that however downtrodden or sick, individuals have survived (and in some cases even thrived). They have taken steps, summoned up resources, and coped. We need to know what they have done, how they have done it, what they have learned from doing it, what resources (inner and outer) were available in their struggle to surmount their troubles . . . as helpers we must tap into that work, elucidate it, find and build on its possibilities. (pp. 171–172)

PROFESSIONAL GROWTH ACTIVITY: A MIRACLE DAY

Next, choose a day in the upcoming week to perform your research. Before going to bed, find a quiet place and ask yourself the Miracle Question, "While I sleep tonight, a miracle will take place, and my problem will be solved. Upon waking in the morning, I'll be aware that something is different. How will I know that a miracle has taken place?"

- How would you like to see this miracle unfold in your life?
- What do you know will be different?
- Who will be the first to notice the change in you?
- What will you be doing that is different?
- What are your physical and emotional responses while contemplating these questions?

Finally, upon waking in the morning try "acting as if" the miracle occurred while you slept and your problem has been solved. For the entire day, and as best as you are able, experience and notice any changes, as if your life were completely on track. At the conclusion of the day and your research experience, discuss your "findings" with a partner.

PROFESSIONAL GROWTH ACTIVITY: READINESS RULER

As a personal research experience to better understand the development of "preferred realities," decide on a problem in your life that you wish to solve and is in your power to do so.

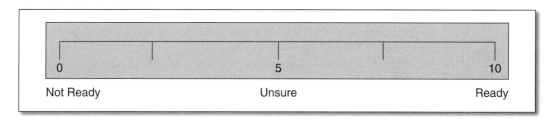

First, consider yourself in relationship to your problem:

- On a scale from 0 to 10, with 0 indicating that you are not ready to make a change, and 10 indicating that you are completely ready, where would you place yourself on the Readiness Ruler for making a change toward solving your problem?
- How would you like to be able to rate your readiness for change?
- What would indicate to you that you are moving toward your desired rating?

PROFESSIONAL GROWTH ACTIVITY: ELICITING A PREFERRED LIFE

In triads, rotate between the following roles:

Client

- Role-play the "essence" of a client or individual you are struggling with.

Counselor

- Elicit and build a preferred life beginning with one of the preferred life questions (refer to Table 7.1). Remember to elicit predicted events, cognitions, actions, and relationships (even to a small degree).

Observer

- Provide feedback on counselor's strengths and windows of opportunity (e.g., strengths, values, ambivalence).

COUNSELOR INTERVIEW & REFLECTION GUIDE

Contracted Change: A Preferred Life

Focus	Intervention
Solution Efforts	*Exceptions* "When would you say the problem had less influence on you? How do you explain this?" "What is different about you during those times when the problem doesn't occur or has less influence? What are you doing differently? What advice are you giving yourself? What is happening differently around you?" "What do you do so that you don't have this problem then? Where did you get the idea to do it differently at those times? Whose idea was it to do it that way?"

Focus	Intervention
	"Do you think this (problem/struggle) should speak for you or do you think it would be better for you to speak for yourself? How will others know that this decision is becoming clearer for you?"
	Unique Outcomes
	"What do you do to keep the problem at bay when you need to? How were you able to weaken the influence of the problem?"
	"When does the problem have less influence on you? What is your guess about why?"
	"Has there ever been a time when the problem might have occurred but didn't? How were you able to do that then? What was different about you at that time?"
	"Who is in your corner regarding your efforts to reduce the influence the problem has on you and those around you? What advise might they provide?"
Miracle, Dream, & Future	*The Miracle*
	"Suppose that when you go to sleep tonight, a miracle occurs, and because you were sleeping, you didn't know it happened. The miracle solved the problem that brought you here. When you wake up in the morning, what clues will you see that lead you to discover that this miracle has taken place?"
	"What else would be different?"
	"What would you notice in the advice you give yourself?"
	"Who would be the first to notice that something had changed?"
	The Dream
	"Suppose that tonight while you are sleeping you have a dream. In this dream you discover the answers and resources you need to solve the problem that you are concerned about right now. When you wake up tomorrow, you may or may not remember your dream; however, you do notice that you are different. As you go about your day, how will you know that you discovered or developed skills and resources necessary to solve your problem?"
	"What else would be different?"
	"What will be the first small bit of evidence that you did this?"
	"Who will be the first to notice and what will they see different in you?"
The Road Ahead	*The Future*
	"Imagine yourself in the future when the problem is no longer a problem. Tell me where you are, what you are doing and saying, and what others around you are doing and saying?"
	"What else would be different?"

(Continued)

(Continued)

Focus	Intervention
Building a Readiness	*Video Talk* "If I were to *watch* you during the time when a miracle was occurring, what behaviors would I see you doing differently?" "What *advice* would you be giving yourself (cognitions)?" "What *would* we see you feeling (emotion)?" *Mind Mapping* "What is your theory about how you were able to do that as you think about the miracle/future? How do you account for these changes?" "What advice will you be giving yourself when the changes you are talking about begin to occur, even just a bit?" "How will you be able to stay on track in spite of all the distractions?" *Intention of Change* "What will you notice in yourself and those around you as you get more comfortable with 'idea' of the changes we talked about today?" *Strengths of Change* "What is there about you, what strong points that we have discussed or that you know about yourself, that could help you succeed in making this change? Who else knows this and could help in this change?" *Hypothetical Change* "Suppose that you did succeed and are looking back at the change now. What most likely is it that worked? How did it happen?" "What obstacles were you able to overcome and how?" "Suppose that this one big obstacle weren't there. If that obstacle were removed, then how might you go about making the change?" "Clearly you are feeling very discouraged about this. Use your imagination. If you were to try again, what might be the best way to try?"

Understanding Goals

You know more than you think you know . . . at an appropriate time, in an appropri-
ate place, your unconscious mind will let your conscious mind know something that
you already know, but don't know that you know.

–Milton Erickson

Assisting clients in conceptualizing their futures apart from the deficit language typically used to describe their problems requires a concerted effort from the counselor.
Although the questions listed in the previous chapter elicit a different set of options in
responding to life challenges, it can be quite normal when people first think about change
to view the process of counseling as resulting merely in the absence their problem, rather
than then the addition of something else. For example, when asked, "What might be a
sign that things are getting better," an individual might typically respond, "When I worry
less and don't get quite as upset as I am now." Life satisfaction is merely the absence of
pain, discomfort, and life troubles. Lent and Lopez (2002) explained that the presenting
problems of individuals and families often (though not always) reflect a significant negative life event (e.g., loss, school failure, trauma) that has diminished their sense of well-
being beyond their typical affective range, as well as their overall sense of coping
efficacy. They classified clients' motivations for self-initiated counseling into two
broad categories: (1) a desire for symptom relief and (2) a desire for growth. The first represents change as *either/or* ("either I have symptom relief, or I do not"). Although significant to client motivations, it ignores the *process* of change. The second category
visualizes growth beyond the relief of symptoms, with an emphasis on overall life satisfaction. Traditional modernist approaches would illustrate these two categories as the
development of short-term (symptom relief) and long-term (life satisfaction) goals where
the attainment of one (short-term goals) would warrant efforts toward the second (long-
term goals). This is consistent with a linear perspective of human change.

Strength-centered counselors envision these two categories of motivations as occurring
simultaneously. The first is no more important than the second when the goals of counseling highlight the struggles of change as well as the outcomes. All goals are client generated and embody the following assumptions.

1. *Change is inherently difficult.* Efforts toward symptom relief and life satisfaction require overcoming growing levels of emotional discomfort and cognitive dissonance. This is the struggle embodied in the change process and the emphasis of strength-centered counseling.

2. *Strengths provide ballast in the rough waters of life and change.* Incorporating clients' strengths with the goals and small steps identified toward change provide stability to link the known (strengths) with the unknown (anticipated actions).

3. *Even the smallest stone creates a ripple.* Clients and families are capable of developing and contemplating small steps toward change. Discouragement and clinical hesitation occur when people perceive counseling goals as too large and the steps toward change as too long.

Incorporating the categories of client motivations with the above assumptions requires a shift (for clients and counselors) toward a process rather than a purely outcome focus. This is consistent with a nonlinear perspective of human change. The activity below is designed to assist with experiencing this shift.

Activity: Change as a Process

Step 1

- Identify a personal habit you wish to change (e.g., quit smoking, increase exercise, lose weight)
- On a sheet of paper draw a line across the page. On one end describe a discouraging habit and the impact on your life. On the other end, describe the actions that represent when this habit is successfully changed.

Step 2

- Above the line connecting the extremes of change, write out those things you will need to overcome to make changing this habit possible.
- Below the line, write down what you know about yourself that might unwittingly sabotage the above efforts.

Step 3

- With a learning partner, discuss the experience of initially viewing change as two extremes and then in reference to the complexities between the two extremes.
- How might this experience relate to the difficulties of change experienced by others and your role as a counselor?

It is important that strength-centered counselors acknowledge the difficulty of perceiving change beyond the immediate struggle while remaining focused on a collaborative discovery of what will be, rather than what has been. In reference to the client statements outlined in the chapter's opening paragraph, a strength-centered counselor might elicit this shift by responding, *"It sounds like your first thoughts of change are about the absence of what has been most troubling for you. This makes sense; I am wondering what you might be feeling instead of worry? How are the things you tell yourself different from those times that you do worry?"*

The questions in Table 8.1 seek to elicit specific action steps with an implied appreciation of the process associated with lifestyle changes. These steps identified by clients and families need to be translated into goals that are specific, positive, personal, and grounded in strengths.

Table 8.1   Eliciting Specific Action Steps

Goal Criteria	Focus Questions
Specific and Achievable	"And how will you (others) know when things are moving in the right direction?" "We often know it is going to rain before rain occurs. What will be the first signs that change is about to occur?"
Positively Framed	"Sounds like you would prefer to be less depressed and more what _____?"
Personal Ownership	"What will be different about you that will contribute to things getting more on track?"
Grounded in Strengths	"And what strengths will you need to tap into to make this (change) possible?"

SCALING STEPS OF ACTION

W. R. Miller and Rollnick (2002) utilized scaling questions to assist counselors and clients in visualizing and prioritizing clinical change. The questions in Table 8.2 break desired changes down into smaller and more achievable steps. This places the counseling goals along a continuum where change is viewed as a process of incremental actions rather than as an "either/or occurrence." Strength-centered counseling seeks to discover the smallest step that clients and families consider reasonable toward symptom relief and life satisfaction. Further, an Action Plan Worksheet can be used with clients and families to assist with translating language to action (see Appendix A).

As stated earlier, tailoring action steps to a client/family stage of readiness can improve the likelihood of successful counseling outcomes. In reference to the stage of change model (Prochaska, DiClemente, & Norcross, 1992), this may include matching goals to a

Table 8.2	Scaling Action Steps	

"On a scale of 1 to 10, with 10 meaning things are completely on track and 1 meaning not at all on track, where would you put yourself today?"

"Where would you like to be on the scale . . . what would you settle for? From where you are today, what would be a very first step toward what you would settle for? How would you recognize that this was occurring for you?"

"When the number on the scale is improved by one point, what will be going in your life, even just a little bit, that is not going on now? What would be a small step indicating to you that you are moving in this direction?"

"Of the steps you mentioned, which do you have confidence that you can accomplish between now and the next time we meet? If not right now, which would you be willing to think more about and pay attention to between now and the next time we meet?"

client's current level of readiness while introducing the goals of the next corresponding level: from precontemplation to contemplation, from contemplation to preparation, from preparation to action, and from action to maintenance. Furthermore, tailoring between-session tasks either to match or to invite an increased stage of change readiness is essential for the hard work of counseling. As important as counseling skills are to the change process, they cannot remove the challenges and stressors awaiting clients and families outside the counselor's door. Change is inherently difficult, and assigning tasks beyond the motivational reach of clients can reinforce the enormity of life challenges and provide a deflated hope for the counseling process. A review of goal considerations as well as between-session tasks that *match* and *invite* clients to a "readiness" for therapeutic action is given in Table 8.3. They are designed to provide specific examples of how strength-centered counselors and clients alike can pay attention to even the smallest steps toward counseling goals. Brown and Lent (1997) found that individuals who perceived little progress by the third session of counseling reported no improvement over the entire course of therapy—irrespective of the clinical treatment employed. It is, therefore, important to elicit and provide opportunities for clients and family to recognize how they are reflecting and addressing the adversity in their lives. This not only increases their confidence in tackling current issues but provides a benchmark for marking their success in overcoming future ones.

This struggle between the dangers associated with "doing something different" and the troubles of "doing more of the same" is a key aspect when enhancing the level of motivation with clients (W. R. Miller & Rolnick, 2002). Goal setting from a strength-centered perspective is to assist others in identifying their "preferred ways of being" as well as the struggles embodied between the contemplation of change and the decision to take action. This emphasis counteracts the demoralization that can occur when change along the stages becomes stalled.

| **Table 8.3** | Stages of Change and Action Steps |

Stage of Change	Focus of Action Steps
Precontemplation	**Goal Considerations** • Explore the client's explanatory world • and explore "other" perspectives related to the client's presenting problems • Acknowledge client strengths and provide information as requested by the client/family **Homework** • A matching assignment: "You have good reasons to be concerned and cautious. This is an important decision and I would agree that this is not something that you should necessarily rush into. Going slow right now makes sense, and we can talk more about this next week, if that is all right with you."
Contemplation	**Goal Considerations** • Encourage the client to think about making changes. • Provide an observational homework assignment (e.g., "What do you notice happen that makes the situation better or worse?") • Acknowledge the ambivalence associated with change and the importance of cautiousness when planning action steps. **Homework** • A matching assignment: "Between now and the next time we meet, I would like you to observe, so that you can describe to me next time, what happened in your life that you want to see continue to happen." • An inviting assignment: "Between now and the next time we meet, choose a day and pretend that the miracle we discussed has occurred for just that day. Do this to the fullest extent you are able and make note of the differences during the day."
Preparation	**Goal Considerations** • Identify clear goals that are framed in the positive, are specific and achievable, are within the ownership of the client, and are grounded in the client. • Assist with prioritizing the initial steps for change and invite clients to set a timetable for initiating change. **Homework** • A matching assignment: "Between now and the next time we meet, notice the small steps we reviewed (summarize) and continue, as much as you possibly can, to do more of these. Make note of how you manage to keep moving forward as well as of those things that slow you down a bit." • An inviting assignment: "Between now and the next time we meet, when you are in a situation where the problem is likely to occur, think/do something different from what you usually do and make note of this."

(Continued)

Table 8.3	(Continued)

Stage of Change	Focus of Action Steps
Action and Maintenance	**Goal Considerations** • Support successful efforts of change while eliciting "how they were able to accomplish small changes while keeping the problem at bay." • Predict and normalize relapses/setbacks as normal and common occurrences of change and any personal journey of discovery. • Identify contingency plans in response to high-risk situations that may impede the planned action steps (e.g., going home for the holidays). **Homework** • A matching assignment: "Between now and the next time we meet, make note, as much as you possibly can, of how you continue to keep things on track as well as how you overcome those daily distracters to your overall well-being." • An inviting assignment: "What might be some indicators that you can pay attention to that would predict that counseling might be nearing an end?"

FOLLOW-UP SUGGESTIONS

It is essential that time be allocated for the counselor and client to reflect on the influence of between-session assignments. For the strength-centered counselor, reflecting on the unique qualities and strengths a client/family embrace in standing up to life's difficulties can be an empathically powerful response. Reflection time not only demonstrates your sincere interest in their well-being, but also allows clients/families to know that you know more than just what the challenges are. They know that you know who they are as people and who they hope to become.

In assisting clients in reflecting on between-session changes, utilizing scaling questions or a series of focused change questions can translate initial impressions to specific actions as well as unrecognized strengths. Subsequent sessions also provide opportunities to allow clients to determine how their counseling experiences are consistent with what they wish different in their lives. This can be a direct inquiry of "whether the differences you are noticing in yourself align with your hopes for counseling" as well as "whether there are any other changes they would wish to see occur." Because the change process from this approach is viewed as ever-changing, unpredictable, and client-centered, it is important to check in with clients and families about their satisfaction with the counseling process, how counseling might better address their hopes and life preferences, and the time frame both between sessions as well as the eventual length of counseling itself, trying to gauge the nonlinear process of termination (see Table 8.4).

| **Table 8.4** | Follow-Up Scaling and Focused Change Questions | |

Follow-Up Scaling Questions on Change	*Follow-Up Focused Change Questions*
"On a scale of 1 to 10, with 10 meaning things are completely on track and 1 meaning not at all on track, where would you put yourself today compared to the last time we met?" • "What is your theory about this?" • "Of those differences that appeared helpful for you, what is your guess about how you were able to do this?" • "What have you learned about yourself that has contributed to these differences?" "Because this is an average, you likely had some days (or moments) better than others. Tell me about those and the differences you noticed."	"What occurred between the last time we met that you would wish to see continue? What do you believe might have been partly responsible for this?" "What personal strengths were you aware of this past week? How do you see this making a difference? What did you need to overcome for this to occur, even just a little bit?" "What is the next step for you?" "Is there anything else you would wish to explore in counseling that might be helpful for you?"

THE THEORY OF HOLES

The essence of a strength-centered interview is to empower individuals to envision "something else occurring" in response to the problems and struggles they enter counseling to overcome. The goals of counseling become secondary to the cooperative exploration where clients, rather than counselors, have the last word on what they need to improve their lives. Because the conversation of change is far more important than the desired outcome, strength-centered counselors need to fight the temptation to give advice or soothe a client's discomfort. This has a tendency to reduce the ambivalence needed to appreciate the struggle associated with personal change and implies little faith in people's ability to visualize and manage the direction of their lives. Ultimately, it places the counselor's desires for clients over those clients have for themselves.

From a strength-centered stance, it is important that counselors do not attempt to *motivate* clients by arguing, persuading, or challenging individuals and/or families toward a plan of action believed to be "in their best interest." This not only implies that counselors somehow know more about client lives than clients themselves, as recently stated, but can place clients in a position of defending the status quo in reaction to counselors inadvertently pushing for change. Often, perceived resistance that a counselor has toward a client is more about the clinical bias of the counselor and not the motivation level of his or her client. It is professionally fatiguing, clinically unproductive, and can naturally lead to clients terminating counseling services. In light of these dangers, it is recommended that strength-centered counselors remember the first law of holes: When you find yourself in one, stop digging.

PROFESSIONAL GROWTH ACTIVITY: ROLE-PLAY CONTRACTED CHANGE

To gain a more concrete understanding of Contracted Change, work with two other counselors to role-play the sequence of steps below:

- Appreciating the Struggle
- Identifying the Dichotomy of Strengths
- Building a Preferred Life (using either the Miracle Question, the Dream Question, or the Future Question)
- Understanding the Road Ahead (with Video Talk and/or Mind Mapping)
- Building a Readiness (using the Readiness Questions)

Take turns playing *Helpee*, *Helper*, and *Observer* while making note of the language and atmosphere created with initiating strength-centered therapeutic conversations. Furthermore, you may wish to record (video or audio) both the role-play session and peer feedback for later review.

Reflective Questions: Experience Contracted Change

Consider the following:

- Who holds the energy in the room—client or counselor?
- What strengths do you recognize in the client in the video?
- What is the dichotomy of those same strengths for this client?
- Practice the strength-centered language in reflecting strengths to a client.
- Practice questions for eliciting from the client his or her own strengths.
- Consider other possible directions the counselor could have taken.

PROFESSIONAL GROWTH ACTIVITY: ACTION STEPS

In triads, rotate among the following roles:

Client

- Revisit previous life struggle or difficulty

Counselor

- Elicit readiness and action steps
- Take a break and discuss with observer the client's stage of change and decide on either a matching assignment or an inviting one

Observer

- Provide feedback about counselor strengths and windows of opportunity (e.g., strengths, values, ambivalence)

COUNSELOR INTERVIEW & REFLECTION GUIDE

Contracted Change: Understanding Goals

Focus	Intervention
Scaling Action Steps	Scaling "On a scale of 1 to 10, with 10 meaning things are completely on track and 1 meaning not at all on track, where would you put yourself today?" "Where would you like to be on the scale . . . what would you settle for? From where you are today, what would be a very first step toward what you would settle for? How would recognize that this was occurring for you?" "When the number on the scale is improved by one point, what will be going in your life, even just a little bit, that is not going on now? What would be a small step indicating to you that you are moving in this direction?" "Of the steps you mentioned, which do you have confidence that you can accomplish between now and the next time we meet? If not right now, which would you be willing to think more about and pay attention to between now and the next time we meet?"
Follow-Up Sessions	Follow-Up Through Scaling "On a scale of 1 to 10, with 10 meaning things are completely on track and 1 meaning not at all on track, where would you put yourself today since the last time we met?" "What is your theory about this?" "Of those differences that appeared helpful for you, what is your guess about how you were able to do this?" "What have you learned about yourself that has contributed to these differences?" Follow-Up Through Change Awareness "What occurred since the last time we met that you would wish to see continue? What do you believe might have been partly responsible for this?" "What personal strengths were you aware of this past week? How do you see these making a difference? What did you need to overcome for this to occur, even just a little bit?" "What is the next step for you?" "Is there anything else you would wish to explore in counseling that might be helpful for you?"

Phase 3: Developed Lifestyle

Understanding Personal Wellness
    Integrating Strengths and Wellness
    Introducing Wellness
    Envisioning Wellness

Practicing Personal Preferences
    Practicing Wellness
    Maintaining Preferences

Strength Centeredness: An Integrated Model

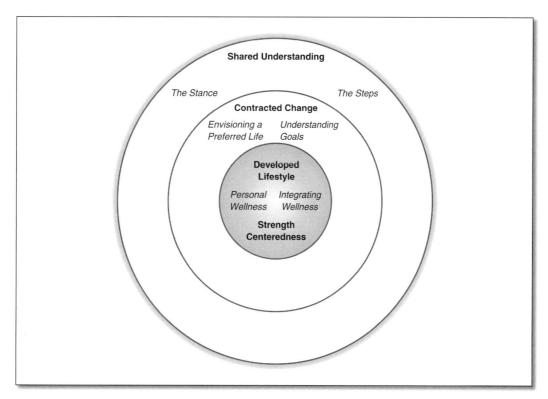

Understanding Personal Wellness

Wellness is the next natural step forward in our destiny and the advancement of humankind. By extending your years of strength and wellness, you can accomplish those things you really want to accomplish.

–Paul Zane Pilzer (2002)

Sue and Sue (1999) noted that Western psychotherapies emphasize individuals in isolation, a linear or direct cause-effect orientation to the world, and a distinction between physical and mental well-being. The deliberate integration of the mind with the body in the counseling process is consistent with the nonlinear nature of change central to postmodernism and the intent of strength-centered counseling. This mind–body connection recognizes that your thoughts, emotions, and behavior directly influence your health and life satisfaction. The truth is, most people are rather oblivious of the small stress indicators and do not begin to take notice until they become impossible to avoid. Headaches, back pain, restlessness, indigestion, edginess, fatigue, forgetfulness, and constant worry are all symptoms that can arise as added life demands begin to accumulate (see Table 9.1). In fact, Veninga and Spradley (1981) defined stress as any additional demand made upon a person. The difficulty of balancing these demands not only can intensify normal life struggles (e.g., career, relationships, and parenting) but can also push through the surface as signs of stress, like weeds breaking through a sidewalk. Far too often well-meaning counselors target these signs as counseling goals while ignoring the struggle that produced them. This also ignores counselors' and clients' opportunities to bring light to existing personal strengths and recognition to forgotten resources.

Incorporating wellness into strength-centered counseling is an attempt, therefore, to recruit the self-healing capacities of the body while emphasizing the interdependent nature of mental, physical, and spiritual aspects of the human experience. By understanding how clients perceive their wellness, counseling goals can be developed that address presenting concerns and also reflect a lifestyle designed for well-being, longevity, and overall health. The activity below will help you to better appreciate these interrelationships in your own life.

Table 9.1	Signs of Stress

Physical: Headaches, indigestion, stomachaches, sweaty palms, sleep difficulties, dizziness, back pain, tight neck/shoulders, racing heart, restlessness, tiredness, ringing in the ears

Behavioral: Excess smoking, bossiness, compulsive gum chewing, critical of others, grinding of teeth at night, overuse of alcohol, compulsive eating, inability to get things done

Emotional: Crying, anxiety, boredom, edginess, powerlessness, feeling overwhelmed, anger, loneliness, unhappiness without apparent reason, difficulty in finding pleasure, easily upset

Cognitive: Trouble thinking clearly, forgetfulness, lack of creativity, memory loss, inability to make decisions, runaway thoughts, constant worry, loss of sense of humor

Activity: A Cause of Stress

Part 1:

- Take out a sheet of paper and a pencil
- Draw a vertical line down the middle of the paper.
- In the *left* column, list the five or six most important things in your life.

Part 2:

- In the *right* column, determine the percentage of time you devote to each of the items listed. *Note:* you cannot surpass 100%
- Rank order the list from most to least important

Part 3:

Discuss your reaction to this activity with a learning partner, reviewing the following questions:

Stress

- What strikes you about this experience?
- What impact do the discrepancies between your values and your time have on you? On others?
- What signs of stress might represent this struggle for you (see Table 9.1)?

Lifestyle

- How might stress reflect lifestyle patterns/decisions for you?
- What are some guesses on how you might attain "better balance" when thinking about reducing the impact of these symptoms?

The degree of discrepancy between those activities that are most important to us and the amount of time we perceive each deserves can create increased levels of daily stress and life dissatisfaction. Over time, this impacts energy levels (fatigue), the ability to fight disease (immune systems), and mood (depression–anxiety). There is a Far Side cartoon (Gary Larson, 1985) that depicts a pilot looking frantically at the co-pilot and shouting, "*The fuel light's on, Frank! We're all going to die! . . . We're all going to die! . . . Wait, wait . . . Oh, my mistake—that's the intercom light.*" The ability to shift perspectives and think holistically is quite difficult when there is a perceived loss of altitude. People are weighed down by immediate life stressors as well as a lifestyle contributing to these stressors. Articulating counseling goals within the context of one's overall wellness assists with connecting present concerns and expectations for counseling to a larger view of oneself. This holistic perspective interprets the process of change as a statement of balance regarding the interplay of life areas, rather than as remediating a deficit in the context of a single aspect of life. Counseling goals become intertwined with both the preferences clients have for themselves (see Phase 2) and lifestyle changes that impact personal well-being and life satisfaction.

INTEGRATING STRENGTHS AND WELLNESS

A variety of holistic models have been proposed to assist with better understanding the dynamic and interdependent aspects of the body, mind, and spirit in relation to lifestyle choices focused on longevity and well-being; however, most models have little empirical evidence to support their recommendations. The model below, developed by Myers and Sweeney (2005, 2008), provides a holistic perspective based on structural equation modeling of a large data set based on The Wheel of Wellness, an earlier theoretical model based on a review of cross-disciplinary health and quality-of-life research and life satisfaction outcomes (see Figure 9.1). Both models share a theoretical foundation in Adlerian psychology where the self, as indivisible, is central to understanding human behavior (Ansbacher & Ansbacher, 1967), Sweeney and Myers's Indivisible Self Wellness Model highlights a single higher-order Indivisible Self factor and the interplay of five core, second-order factors of wellness: Creative Self, Coping Self, Social Self, Physical Self, and Essential Self. Furthermore, each core area consists of third-order factors that are characteristics of wellness and of healthy persons, necessary for high-level and holistic wellness.

From a strength-centered perspective every counseling encounter embodies a need to overcome immediate life challenges as well as adjust ongoing patterns of personal wellness reflected in the struggles, experience, and life decisions of clients and families impacting their overall well-being and life satisfaction. Therapies that focus solely on problem resolution often fail to directly address lifestyle patterns that represent health beyond the absence of the initial concerns. By understanding human struggles through a perspective of strengths, counselors are able to identify those qualities and skills needed to address clients' initial concerns as well as lifestyle choices for increasing overall personal wellness. For example, identifying the need for temperance (a protection against excess) not only establishes goals for initial concerns (e.g., standing up to the demands of others, accepting personal limitations), but also highlights ongoing coping patterns and life responding skills. The strengths needed to stand up to adversity are the same strengths needed to

| Figure 9.1 | The Indivisible Self |

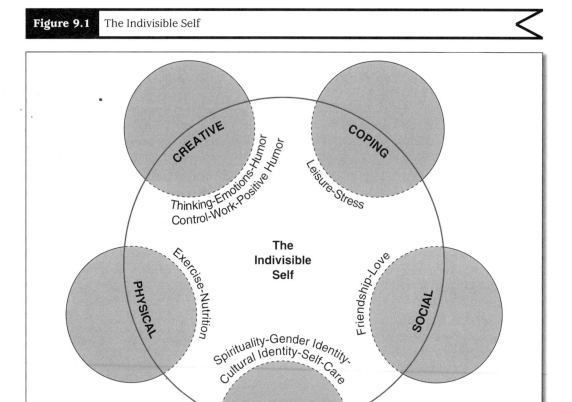

Source: Sweeney, T. J., & Myers, J. E. (2003, 2009). *The indivisible self: An evidence-based model of wellness.* Reprinted with permission of the authors.

increase optimal health and well-being. Table 9.2 highlights the interplay between the Indivisible Self Wellness model and personal strength awareness.

The following is intended is a brief overview of each wellness area, including a brief definition, related skills, and a primary strength category. As will be reviewed later, having an understanding of the wellness components is an essential aspect of a wellness counseling interview (Myers & Sweeney, 2004; Sweeney & Myers, 2005). This shared knowledge between counselors and clients can remind us of the purpose of counseling: to establish a relationship that seeks to restore a sense of connectedness, indestructibility, and control in one's life (Cassell, 1978). It also provides a map on which to connect clients' struggles

Table 9.2 The Indivisible Self (Sweeney & Myers, 2009) and Strength Awareness

Strength Characteristics	Wisdom and Knowledge (Pursuit of Learning)	Temperance (Protection against Excess)	Humanity and Love (Befriending Others)	Courage (Exercise of Will)	Transcendence (Spiritual Connection)
Strength Qualities	Creativity, Curiosity, Open-mindedness, Learning, Perspective	Forgiveness, Humility, Accepting Prudence, Cautious, Disciplined	Caring, Kindness, Generosity Social intelligence, Empathic	Valor, Persistence, Integrity Honesty, Responsible, Vitality	Appreciative, Grateful, Hopeful, Faithful, Optimistic, Playful, Spiritual
Wellness Area	*Creative Self*	*Coping Self*	*Social Self*	*Physical Self*	*Essential Self*
Life Skills (Characteristics of Healthy Persons: Third-Order Wellness Factors)	• Problem Solving • Sense of Humor • Sense of Control • Emotional Awareness • Work	• Stress Management • Self-Worth • Realistic Beliefs • Leisure	• Friendship • Love	• Exercise • Nutrition • Self-Care	• Spirituality • Gender Identity • Cultural Identity

(Phase 1) with their preferences (Phase 2), as well as with those actions connected to enhancing their overall wellness and well-being (Phase 2).

Creative Self

This factor of wellness encompasses five skill components needed for daily living. The primary strength category is *Wisdom and Knowledge* illustrated in the following:

1. *Problem Solving and Creativity:* The need to know, learn, and organize while maintaining a sense of curiosity and wonder

2. *Sense of Humor:* The ability to use humor and laughter for the release of tension, boosting the immune system, stimulating circulation, aiding in digestion, and releasing of endorphins that can enhance mood

3. *Sense of Control:* The capacity to influence life's events as well as actively managing stress and building psychological hardiness with regular exercise and nutrition

4. *Emotional Awareness and Coping:* The ability to experience and express emotions fully while aware of the synchronous relationship between thoughts, emotions, and physical responses

5. *Work:* Work provide opportunities for pleasurable experiences, a sense of accomplishment, financial reward, and stimulating challenges

Coping Self

This area of wellness highlights skills needed to respond effectively to the challenges of life. The primary strength category is *Temperance* and the skills associated with this wellness strength are as follows:

1. *Skills of Stress Management:* The ability to identify stressors in one's life and to utilize strategies for reducing or minimizing their physical, emotional, and cognitive impact

2. *Skills of Self-Worth:* The ability to demonstrate excitement over new challenges, a desire to be in harmony with others, a pursuit of self-awareness and actualization, and strong internal locus of control and decision making ability

3. *Skills Toward Realistic Beliefs:* The willingness to see life "as it is" while accepting oneself as "imperfect"

4. *Skills of Leisure:* The commitment to activities (physical, social, intellectual, volunteer, and creative) that have a positive effect on self-esteem and overall perceived wellness

Social Self

This factor includes components of friendship and love that enhance the quality and length of one's life. The primary strength category is *Humanity and Love* in relationship to the following components:

1. *Friendship:* The innate drive for belonging and incorporating all the skills needed to connect with others (individually or in a community) without a sexual or familial commitment

2. *Love:* The experience of a healthy love relationship, including the ability to (a) be intimate, trusting, and self-disclosing; (b) receive as well as express affection with significant others; (c) convey nonpossessive caring that respects uniqueness; (d) establish enduring, stable intimate relationships; (e) exhibit concern for the nurturance and growth of others; and (f) meet the sexual and physical needs of touch and closeness

Physical Self

This factor incorporates a commitment toward exercise, nutrition, and overall self-care skills. The primary strength category is *Courage;* it embodies a lifestyle that includes the following:

1. *Exercise:* The discipline to maintain the skills needed for an active lifestyle that can increase strength, self-esteem, and cognitive functioning, and that are essential for preventing disease

2. *Nutrition:* The understanding of how food and one's health, mood, and performance are interrelated

3. *Self-Care:* The skills needed to take responsibility for one's personal habits as well as overall wellness

Essential Self

This factor embodies one's existential sense of meaning, purpose, and hopefulness about life and includes spirituality and gender/cultural identity. The primary strength category is *Transcendence;* it is reflected in the following:

1. *Spirituality:* The awareness of a being or force that transcends the material aspects of life and gives a deep sense of wholeness and connectedness to the universe. Spirituality incorporates optimism and a "buffer" against stress that can increase life satisfaction and longevity. Myers (2003) proposed that spirituality may be defined as the capacity and tendency present in all human beings to find and construct meaning about life and existence and to move toward personal growth, responsibility, and relationships with others.

2. *Gender/Cultural Identity:* The understanding of how filters developed through life experiences are viewed and influence one's relationship to others, oneself, and life in general.

INTRODUCING WELLNESS

> *The baby fish said to the mama fish, what's water?*
>
> –Author unknown

As understood by Myers, Sweeney, and Witmer (2000), personal wellness is defined as a

> way of life oriented toward optimal health and well-being, in which body, mind, and spirit are integrated by the individual to live life more fully within the human and natural community. Ideally, it is the optimum state of health and well-being that each individual is capable of achieving. (p. 252)

A wellness perspective also promotes a belief in the resiliency and self-healing properties of people to cope with the ups and downs of life. Well-being translates into more than the absence of depression, anxiety, anger, and stress. It becomes an active and continuous process of embracing personal strengths and individual qualities of resiliency in standing up against personal, social, and cultural adversity.

Wellness can be introduced in a variety ways specific to the unique qualities of the client or family, the counseling setting, and the level of comfort and training of the counselor. The essential thrust at this point in strength-centered counseling is the introduction of wellness as part of a broader exploration of the presenting issues, concerns, and/or struggles. In contrast to an illness ideology where mental health services focus on remediating deficits and symptoms, one that highlights strengths while perceiving change as a natural part of life and maturing, embodies hope. The following nicely describes the value of this introduction to clients and families.

> If we anticipate that we will be working with a client over time, then we should introduce the wellness model and strategies early on in the counseling relationship. After taking both classes I am in complete agreement because I think it provides another level of support and empowerment to offer the client. I think it also gives the counselor more tools to work with and could reveal multiple points of view of the client and their strengths. In my future work I would like to work with the various wellness survey/instruments we used in the Wellness Counseling course in conjunction with the Inventory of Strengths Survey and the Strength Cards to help me better identify my clients' preferences and needs. –Sarah S.

Table 9.3 shows steps for assisting strength-centered counselors with introducing the idea of wellness in the context of developing counseling goals and action steps. Each step

Table 9.3 Introducing Wellness

Introducing Wellness	Eliciting Personal Wellness Meaning
Step 1: Orientation to the Idea of Wellness "I feel like I am getting a pretty good idea of what you wish to accomplish during our time together. Often, counseling goals can reflect decisions that not only address your initial concerns, but also work at increasing your overall well-being and life satisfaction as well as preventing future illness. Would it be all right with you if we take time to explore how the counseling goals we identified might also consider ongoing lifestyle decisions?"	"What does wellness mean to you as you think about your life now?"
Step 2: Presenting the Model "The following wellness model represents a way to look at ourselves as an interplay among our essential, creative, coping, physical, and social life aspects" (show model and briefly define each core component). "Before we explore these areas more fully, it might be helpful to start with your initial impressions."	"What strikes you about the wellness model?" "As you consider the main headings in the circles of wellness, what things come to mind?" "What areas of wellness to you believe might assist with successfully addressing your expectations for counseling?"

is followed by strategic questions designed to elicit a dialogue of personal meaning around one's overall sense of wellness. With a learning partner (or in a journal) note your reactions as you reflect on your personal meaning of wellness.

ENVISIONING WELLNESS

The model specifies that wellness is the cumulative effect of several factors associated with human behavior and efforts to meet life's demands.

–Hattie, Myers, and Sweeney (2004)

The interview guide in Table 9.4 is designed to facilitate clients' detailed exploration and growing understanding of their experience of personal wellness across the five self areas and

Table 9.4	Interview Guide: Exploring Wellness	

Overall Wellness	*On a scale of 1 to 10, identify the number that best reflects your overall wellness and your satisfaction.*
Overall Wellness	1 2 3 4 5 6 7 8 9 10
Satisfaction	1 2 3 4 5 6 7 8 9 10
Essential Self (Transcendence)	*On a scale of 1 to 10, identify the number that best reflects your overall spiritual wellness and your satisfaction with your spiritual wellness.*
Perception	1 2 3 4 5 6 7 8 9 10
Satisfaction	1 2 3 4 5 6 7 8 9 10
Strengths	*What strengths appear to* assist *or to* hinder *your satisfaction in this wellness area?*
Coping Self (Temperance)	*On a scale of 1 to 10, identify the number that best reflects your overall wellness in responding to life's circumstances as well as your satisfaction.*
Managing Stress	Perception: 1 2 3 4 5 6 7 8 9 10
	Satisfaction: 1 2 3 4 5 6 7 8 9 10
Sense of Worth	Perception: 1 2 3 4 5 6 7 8 9 10
	Satisfaction: 1 2 3 4 5 6 7 8 9 10
Realistic Beliefs	Perception: 1 2 3 4 5 6 7 8 9 10
	Satisfaction: 1 2 3 4 5 6 7 8 9 10
Leisure	Perception: 1 2 3 4 5 6 7 8 9 10
	Satisfaction: 1 2 3 4 5 6 7 8 9 10

(Continued)

Table 9.4 (Continued)

Strengths	What strengths appear to assist or to hinder your satisfaction in each component of your Coping Self?
Social Self (Humanity & Love)	On a scale of 1 to 10, identify the number that best reflects your overall wellness in your daily relationships as well as your satisfaction.
Friendships	Perception: 1 2 3 4 5 6 7 8 9 10 Satisfaction: 1 2 3 4 5 6 7 8 9 10
Love	Perception: 1 2 3 4 5 6 7 8 9 10 Satisfaction: 1 2 3 4 5 6 7 8 9 10
Strengths	What strengths are appear to assist or to hinder your satisfaction in each component of your Social Self?
Physical Self (Courage)	On a scale of 1 to 10, identify the number that best reflects your overall physical wellness and overall satisfaction.
Exercise	Perception: 1 2 3 4 5 6 7 8 9 10 Satisfaction: 1 2 3 4 5 6 7 8 9 10
Nutrition	Perception: 1 2 3 4 5 6 7 8 9 10 Satisfaction: 1 2 3 4 5 6 7 8 9 10
Strengths	What strengths appear to assist or to hinder your satisfaction in each component of your Physical Self?
Creative Self (Wisdom & Knowledge)	On a scale of 1 to 10, identify the number that best reflects your overall wellness in your skills for daily living as well as your satisfaction.
Problem Solving & Creativity	Perception: 1 2 3 4 5 6 7 8 9 10 Satisfaction: 1 2 3 4 5 6 7 8 9 10
Sense of Control	Perception: 1 2 3 4 5 6 7 8 9 10 Satisfaction: 1 2 3 4 5 6 7 8 9 10
Sense of Humor	Perception: 1 2 3 4 5 6 7 8 9 10 Satisfaction: 1 2 3 4 5 6 7 8 9 10
Emotional Awareness & Coping	Perception: 1 2 3 4 5 6 7 8 9 10 Satisfaction: 1 2 3 4 5 6 7 8 9 10
Work	Perception: 1 2 3 4 5 6 7 8 9 10 Satisfaction: 1 2 3 4 5 6 7 8 9 10
Strengths	What strengths appear to assist or to hinder your satisfaction in each component of your Creative Self?

related skill components. Adapted from the work and writings of Jane Myers and Tom Sweeney, this series of questions assists clients with envisioning how personal wellness relates to their initial counseling goals and to the strengths needed to accomplish both. Although the guide utilizes a Likert scale to measure the level of client perception and satisfaction as it relates to each core area of personal wellness, the score is not the focus or purpose. The intent of strength-centered counseling is to facilitate a reflective dialogue where initial concerns and counseling goals are placed, often for the first time, within a broader context of life satisfaction and well-being. In preparation for working through this interview guide with clients, enlist a learning partner (or use your journal) to note your reactions as you reflect on your level of wellness perception and satisfaction with each component area as well as those strengths that assist in some areas and hinder others.

Once you have explored the level of meaning and satisfaction that clients have toward their areas and related components to wellness, linking this to their initial concerns and their actions toward a "preferred life" becomes essential. The bridging, future, and strength questions in Table 9.5 are designed to assist counselors and clients with this clinical transition. Again working with your learning partner (or journal), have a shared

Table 9.5	Envisioning Wellness
Bridging Questions	"As you reflect on your areas of personal wellness, which do you believe might have been partly responsible for the concerns you entered counseling with?"
	"Which wellness areas might have assisted in keeping things from getting worse and your head above water?"
Future Questions	"Often as counseling goals are reached, areas of wellness also shift. Which wellness areas will be different as life becomes more on track? How will they look different then in comparison to now?"
	"Imagine yourself in the future when you feel more in balance with your overall wellness. Tell me where you are, what you are doing and saying, and what others around you are doing and saying."
Strength Questions	"What do you know or are learning about you that will contribute to meeting your counseling and wellness goals successfully?"
	"What other strengths will you need to tap into to overcome the challenges ahead as you begin the work of change?"

conversation about these strategic questions. Note your personal reactions to the inquiry as well as to the entire wellness-oriented interview.

I am also getting the sense of how important wellness for me as the counselor will be when I start working in the field. Just from our brief dyad work over the course of the weekend [seminar] I could feel myself getting tired and drained from listening and interacting so intimately with other people. The first weekend I had a hard time sleeping because I was both excited and mentally rehashing the conversations with my classmates. It made me realize that when I do have a practice of my own I will need to have healthy outlets to address the stress and emotions that might come up for me. The more balanced and centered I am, the better I will be able to help my clients address their own issues with a sense of calm and confidence. –Shelby W.

Shifting to a holistic perspective can be difficult and often counterintuitive for counselors. There is a tendency to become preoccupied with only reducing or removing initial clinical symptoms. This restricted idea of change is embedded in most mental health training programs, adopted by third-party payers, and illustrated in clinical treatment plans where people are reduced to categories so that interventions focused on symptom reduction might be implemented. Understanding and developing counseling goals that consider people in a broader context requires deliberate and concentrated effort by counselors. It is the act of striving to benefit clients and families by establishing therapeutic goals that reflect a larger concern for their overall welfare.

Maturana wrote, "The knowledge of knowledge compels" (1987, p. 245). Linking personal wellness strategies to the clinical planning process provides a context of learning for clients and families where they may thrive, grow, and change beyond their initial expectations. This embodies the moral essence of "beneficence." The wellness interview as outlined in Table 9.4 provides counselors an avenue to advocate for the dignity, welfare, and overall good of their clientele while simultaneously addressing the initial expectations and hopes for counseling.

PROFESSIONAL GROWTH ACTIVITY: CONTEMPLATING COUNSELOR WELLNESS

Part 1

- Working with a learning partner, practice using the interview guide shown in Table 9.4.
- Working with the Envisioning Wellness questions in Table 9.5, review with your partner the experience of the wellness interview.
- Reverse roles.

Part 2

Without a partner, spend a few moments with yourself to consider both the experience of working through the wellness interview guide shown in Table 9.4 and the bridging, future, and strength questions presented in Table 9.5.

How will understanding your own relationship with personal wellness influence your work as a helping professional?

Practicing Personal Preferences

Meditation is not an evasion. It is a serene encounter with reality.

–Thich Nhat Hanh

In her review of practices in cardiac rehabilitation, Meg Wise (2001) concluded that traditional programs relying heavily on medication and cognitive/behavioral interventions for reducing risk patterns have low "adherence rates," compromise long-term success, and do not meet the needs of most patients. She cited the work of Dean Ornish in which individuals participating in a cardiac rehabilitation program that incorporated support groups, counseling, meditation, and an extra-low-fat diet demonstrated a reversal of heart disease with no medication in contrast to individuals in traditional care groups with medication, who had worsened (Gould, Ornish, & Scherwitz, 1995). Based on reviews of outcome studies, Wise finally contended that healing from heart disease is dependent on (a) the level of available social support, (b) the degree of spiritual meaning applied to current life struggles, and (c) the reflective ability of individuals to appreciate the mind–body properties for achieving balance and life harmony. In other words, as Ornish described (1990), healing often had less to do with addressing the improper exchange of oxygen (pumps, valves, and tubes) and more to do with an appreciation of the proper exchange of emotion and spirit. So it is with strength-centered wellness. A narrow focus on symptom reduction not only promotes deficit-based counseling goals but also limits a broader perspective on the interconnectedness between the mind, body, and spirit as it relates to healing and, ultimately, transformation. It also can be a prescription for professional burnout. According to Bertolino and O'Hanlon (2002), "If the lenses through which we look at clients only reveal what's wrong, it's not difficult to see how therapists can become disheartened and hopeless—the same as clients" (p. 257).

PRACTICING WELLNESS

"Lifestyle interventions" that seek to promote this interconnectedness at each level of personal wellness can be found in Table 10.1. Not designed to be inclusive (as that would be beyond the scope of this book), the interventions provide a glimpse into how strength-centered counselors

Table 10.1   Lifestyle Interventions

Strength Characteristics	Wisdom and Knowledge (Pursuit of Learning)	Temperance (Protection Against Excess)	Humanity and Love (Befriending Others)	Courage (Exercise of Will)	Transcendence (Spiritual Connection)
Strength Qualities	Creativity, Curiosity, Open-Mindedness, Learning, Perspective	Forgiveness, Humility, Acceptance, Prudence, Caution, Discipline	Care, Kindness, Generosity Social Intelligence, Empathy	Valor, Persistence, Integrity Honesty, Responsibility, Vitality	Appreciation, Gratitude, Hope, Faith, Optimism, Playfulness, Spirituality
Wellness Area	Creative Self	Coping Self	Social Self	Physical Self	Essential Self
Life Skills	• Problem Solving • Sense of Humor • Sense of Control • Emotional Awareness • Work	• Stress Management • Self Worth • Realistic Beliefs • Leisure	• Friendship • Love	• Exercise • Nutrition • Self Care	• Spirituality • Gender Identity • Cultural Identity
Interventions (Potential)	Finding Humor Creative Avenues Career Counseling	Relaxation Response Mindfulness Meditation & Yoga Cognitive Instruction Volunteerism	Positive Psychology Social Wheel Awareness Wheel	Active Lifestyle Planning Self Care	Prayer Wheel Diversity Insight Gratitude Journal
Suggested Readings	Mikulas (2002). *The Integrative Helper: Convergence of Eastern and Western Traditions.*	Greenberg (2006). *Comprehensive Stress Management* (9th ed.).	Snyder & Lopez (2002). *Handbook of Positive Psychology.*	Sperry, Lewis, Carlson, & Englar-Carlson (2005). *Health Promotion and Health Counseling: Effective Counseling and Psychotherapeutic Strategies.*	Myers & Sweeney (2005). *Counseling for Wellness.*

might highlight lifestyle strategies gleaned from the wellness interview and integrated with expressed client preferences (Phase 2 of strength-centered counseling). Maintaining a holistic window when working through life struggles for both yourself and your clientele not only is a reminder of the difficulty associated with personal change but also illustrates the importance of wellness when promoting the same for others. In this chapter you are invited to experience select personal wellness interventions. These activities might also assist with hanging on to a holistic and strength-centered perspective in a clinical world of pathology and disorder. To take care of all parts of yourself is to fight back the fatigue of your compassion, so that you might continue to make a difference in the lives of others.

Creative Self

This factor of wellness encompasses the daily living skills of problem solving and creativity, humor, control, emotional awareness and coping, and work. The primary strength category is *Wisdom and Knowledge,* and the suggested personal wellness intervention is the use of the Emotional Awareness Guide (adapted from Nunnally, Miller, & Wackman, 1975). Consider a recent interaction where you experienced conflict and/or tension. Fill out Table 10.2 from both your perspective and from the other individual's perspective. Note your reactions and share this with a learning partner (or in a journal).

Table 10.2	Activity A: Emotional Awareness Guide	

My Perspective	Activity A Areas of Awareness	Other Perspective
	Sensing What did I hear or see that contributed to my reaction and discomfort?	
	Thinking How did I interpret this? What did it mean to me that this occurred?	
	Feeling What was I feeling during the interaction? What does this tell me about my own needs?	
	Intention What did I want from the interaction? How clear was I about this?	
	Action How did I respond? What might have said and done that would have been more consistent with my wishes, needs, and intentions?	

Coping Self

This area of wellness highlights skills needed to respond effectively to the challenges of life and encompasses the skills of stress management, self-worth, realistic beliefs, and leisure. The primary strength category is *Temperance*. A suggested personal wellness intervention is Mindfulness, which is the ability to keep your attention focused on the present (see Table 10.3). Breathing is the primary tool to assist in becoming "mindfully aware" of how your body processes thoughts, emotions, and/or tensions. Please share your reactions to the activities in Table 10.3 with a learning partner (or in your journal).

Table 10.3 Activity B and Activity C: Mindfulness

Activity B	Activity C
Choose a focus word, phrase, or short prayer that has special meaning	Take a deep breath and hold it for a few seconds; as you exhale, repeat your focus word
Take a deep breath and hold it for a few seconds. As you exhale, repeat your focus word	Breathe in through your nose and out through your mouth.
Repeat this 10 times as you take note of the changes in your body	Focus on the temperature changes in the air between the inhales and exhales (Nasal Cycle)
	Without judgment or censure, make note of your emerging thoughts and emotions
Process Question	
Can you name a few everyday irritations where this might be useful?	*Process Question*
	How might you apply this experience during your day?

Social Self

This factor includes components of friendship and love that enhance the quality and length of one's life. The primary strength category is *Humanity and Love*. Suggested health interventions are Acts of Kindness and a Gratitude Visit (see Table 10.4). Both are related to the research outcomes of Positive Psychology, which seeks to understand optimal

Table 10.4 Activity D and Activity E: Acts of Kindness and Gratitude Visit

Activity D	Activity E
Acts of Kindness	Gratitude Visit
For a period of one week, perform three acts of kindness daily. Make note of your reactions, and at the end of the week, share these with a learning partner (adapted from Lyubomirsky, Sheldon, & Schkade, 2005)	Write a letter of gratitude to someone and then arrange to visit the person and read the letter aloud to him or her. Do this once a week for 3 weeks and note your reactions. Share these reactions with a learning partner (adapted from Emmons & McCullough, 2003)

human functioning by discovering and promoting the factors that allow individuals and communities to thrive (Seligman & Csikszentmihalyi, 2000).

Physical Self

This factor incorporates a commitment to exercise, nutrition, and overall self-care skills. It can be the most difficult and illustrates the primary strength category of *Courage*. This is essential to developing an active and balanced lifestyle. Consistent with the tenets espoused by William Glasser (1975, 1999), strength-centered counseling contends that people are purposeful and in charge of their lives when change is focused on assisting others with taking responsibility for their future goals. Adapted from *Reality Therapy* (Glasser, 1975) and *Motivational Interviewing* (W. R. Miller & Rollnick, 2002), the following are six steps for developing a plan of commitment toward self-care and physical well-being. Below is an example of how these steps might be applied when initiating steps toward a more active lifestyle. Table 10.5 reviews target areas related to active living, and Table 10.6 articulates steps for developing a plan of

Table 10.5	Activity F: Active Living Target Areas	

Daily Activity	*Regular Exercise*	*Balance*
This may include: • Play active games with children/grandchildren • Walk or bike to work • Climb the stairs rather than ride the elevator • Walk to do errands • Tend to the yard • Park car toward the back of the lot and walk to the office	Regular, scheduled exercise need only be of "moderate intensity" (a brisk walk of 30–60 minutes three to five times a week) The focus is on enjoyment, moderation, and consistency	A complete approach to physical fitness includes all types of body work to improve endurance, strength, and flexibility This may include: • Breathing • Meditation • Massage • Yoga

Table 10.6	Activity G: Action Plan Steps	

Steps	*Focus Questions*
ONE Focus on Current Behavior	• What do you want different now? • What are you doing now that contributes to the problem (e.g., fatigue)? • Tell me about a time when the problem had less influence on your actions? What were you doing differently then?
TWO Assess Current Actions	• Is what you are doing helping or working for you? • Is what you are doing what you wish to be doing? • What would you wish yourself to be doing differently?

(Continued)

Table 10.6   (Continued)

Steps	Focus Questions
THREE Develop an Action Plan	• On a scale of 1 to 10, with 10 meaning you have every confidence that this problem can be solved and 1 meaning no confidence at all, where would you put yourself today? • When the number on the scale is improved by 1 point, what will be going on in your life that is not going on now? What would be a small step indicating to you that you are moving in this direction? • On a scale of 1–10, how much confidence do you have that you can accomplish one of these small steps between now and the next time we meet? Where will you need the number to be in order to move from thinking about change to acting on your contemplations?
FOUR Understand the Plan	• What obstacles might arise to sabotage your best intentions? • How might the courage needed to address this be applied to get you what you want? What other strengths might you need to tap into to address this? • What will you be doing differently when you have succeeded in overcoming these obstacles? What helpful advice will you be providing yourself? • What are the dangers of initiating this plan right now? What will be the first indicators that you are ready to move forward? • If you have begun initiating parts of the plan, what occurred that you would like to see yourself continue to do? What will you need to do differently?
FIVE Benefits and Consequences	• What are the benefits of this plan for you? • Who would be in support of this plan for you and why? • Are the consequences of not initiating this plan enough to overcome the discomfort, fear, and uncertainty of moving forward? If not, what would be?
SIX Mission Statement	• All plans are guided by a mission statement. What will yours be? What are the guiding principles of your plan? Who are the primary participants? • Besides the courage needed to try "something different," what other personal strengths and resources that you know about yourself will be helpful to tap into during the course of your plan?

action. Follow the steps and write out responses to the focus questions as these relate to becoming more physically active. Note your experience and schedule a time to share your reactions with a learning partner one week after completing the steps.

Essential Self

This factor embodies one's existential sense of meaning, purpose, and hopefulness about life and includes spirituality and gender/cultural identity. The primary strength category is *Transcendence* and the selected intervention is the Prayer Wheel. From their research, Russell and Glass (2002) concluded the following with regard to how their participants experienced spirituality:

- It represented a search for meaning and an understanding that provided meaning and peace as to the reason of their lives.
- It did not imply a belief in a force greater than they are, but a force that should be left to individual interpretation.
- It is a powerful concept that is very personal and can represent different things to different people.
- Spirituality and Religion were experienced as two separate concepts that do not always mesh into one.

The Prayer Wheel (Wallis, 1996) can be an effective tool for increasing one's awareness of life's "blessings" and assisting with finding solutions. Choose a period of time during the upcoming week to experience the 8 steps of the Prayer Wheel (Table 10.7). Do so with pen in hand. In your journal or with a learning partner, reflect on the experience and which steps held special meaning for you.

Table 10.7	Activity H: Prayer Wheel	

Components of Prayer	Directions
1. Count your blessings	Write down specific things you are thankful for that day
2. Sing of love	Sing, hum, or listen to a soothing song
3. Request guidance and protection	Ask protection from negative thoughts and deeds of self and others
4. Forgive self and others	Write a statement forgiving self and others for past transgressions
5. Ask for needs	Ask for what you need in your life
6. Ask to be filled with love and inspiration	Write briefly, asking for more positive qualities in your life
7. Listen with pen in hand	After completing the previous steps, sit quietly and write about thoughts, images, or emotions that arise
8. Your will is my will	Encourage yourself to "let go" and trust that you will receive what you most need at this time

MAINTAINING PREFERENCES

Integrating an understanding of human struggles with the language of strengths and the practice of personal wellness, strength-centered counselors offer clients hope and the possibility that they may thrive, grow, and change beyond their immediate life challenges. This chapter has introduced you to lifestyle interventions focusing on further development of specific strengths of each level of personal wellness. Sharing an understanding of how clients perceive their wellness, counseling goals address presenting concerns while reflecting a balanced lifestyle. Further, a counseling approach that highlights the awareness and development of personal strengths bolsters resilience against future adversity.

Presenting concerns often reflect lifestyle decisions around core self aspects (creative, coping, social, physical, and essential). Phase 3 of strength-centered counseling seeks to incorporate these aspects into the planning of therapeutic change with individuals and families. However, working with clients on the development of their core aspects of self can occur during any time in the counseling process. By embracing an expanded perspective of the outcomes of counseling, counselors can travel with others toward extraordinary discoveries beyond the relief of suffering where an increased sense of harmony, fulfillment, and well-being await.

COUNSELOR INTERVIEW & REFLECTION GUIDE

Developed Lifestyle—Understanding Personal Wellness

Focus	Intervention
Introducing Wellness	*Steps to Introducing Wellness* *Step 1: Orientation* "I feel like I am getting a pretty good idea of what you wish to accomplish during our time together. Often, counseling goals can reflect decisions that not only address your initial concerns but also work to increase your overall well-being and life satisfaction as well as avoiding future illness. Would it be all right with you if we take time to explore how the counseling goals we identified might also consider ongoing lifestyle decisions?" • "What does wellness *mean* to you as you think about your life now?" *Step 2: Presenting the Model* "The following wellness model represents a way to look at ourselves as an interplay among our essential, creative, coping, physical, and social life aspects" (show model and briefly define each core component). "Before we explore these areas more fully, it might be helpful to start with your initial impressions."
Envisioning Wellness	• "What strikes you about the wellness model?" • "As you consider the main headings in the circles of wellness, what things come to mind?" • "What areas of wellness to you believe might assist with successfully addressing your expectations for counseling?"

Focus	Intervention	

Overall Wellness	*On a scale of 1 to 10, identify the number that best reflects your overall wellness and your satisfaction.*	
Overall Wellness	1 2 3 4 5 6 7 8 9 10	
Satisfaction	1 2 3 4 5 6 7 8 9 10	

Essential Self (Transcendence)	*On a scale of 1 to 10, identify the number that best reflects your overall spiritual wellness and your satisfaction with your spiritual wellness.*
Perception	1 2 3 4 5 6 7 8 9 10
Satisfaction	1 2 3 4 5 6 7 8 9 10
Strengths	*What strengths appear to* assist *or to* hinder *your satisfaction in this wellness area?*

Coping Self (Temperance)	*On a scale of 1 to 10, identify the number that best reflects your overall wellness in responding to life's circumstances as well as your satisfaction.*
Managing Stress	Perception: 1 2 3 4 5 6 7 8 9 10 Satisfaction: 1 2 3 4 5 6 7 8 9 10
Sense of Worth	Perception: 1 2 3 4 5 6 7 8 9 10 Satisfaction: 1 2 3 4 5 6 7 8 9 10
Realistic Beliefs	Perception: 1 2 3 4 5 6 7 8 9 10 Satisfaction: 1 2 3 4 5 6 7 8 9 10
Leisure	Perception: 1 2 3 4 5 6 7 8 9 10 Satisfaction: 1 2 3 4 5 6 7 8 9 10
Strengths	*What strengths appear to* assist *or to* hinder *your satisfaction in each component of your Coping Self?*

(Continued)

(Continued)

Focus	Intervention		
	Social Self (Humanity & Love)	*On a scale of 1 to 10, identify the number that best reflects your overall wellness in your daily relationships as well as your satisfaction.*	
	Friendships	Perception: 1 2 3 4 5 6 7 8 9 10 Satisfaction: 1 2 3 4 5 6 7 8 9 10	
	Love	Perception: 1 2 3 4 5 6 7 8 9 10 Satisfaction: 1 2 3 4 5 6 7 8 9 10	
	Strengths	*What strengths appear to assist or to hinder your satisfaction in each component of your Social Self?*	
	Physical Self (Courage)	*On a scale of 1 to 10, identify the number that best reflects your overall physical wellness and overall satisfaction.*	
	Exercise	Perception: 1 2 3 4 5 6 7 8 9 10 Satisfaction: 1 2 3 4 5 6 7 8 9 10	
	Nutrition	Perception: 1 2 3 4 5 6 7 8 9 10 Satisfaction: 1 2 3 4 5 6 7 8 9 10	
	Strengths	*What strengths appear to assist or to hinder your satisfaction in each component of your Physical Self?*	
Integrating Wellness	*Creative Self (Wisdom & Knowledge)*	*On a scale of 1 to 10, identify the number that best reflects your overall wellness in your skills for daily living as well as your satisfaction.*	
	Problem Solving & Creativity	Perception: 1 2 3 4 5 6 7 8 9 10 Satisfaction: 1 2 3 4 5 6 7 8 9 10	

Focus	Intervention	
Integrating Wellness	*Creative Self (Wisdom & Knowledge)*	*On a scale of 1 to 10, identify the number that best reflects your overall wellness in your skills for daily living as well as your satisfaction.*
	Sense of Control	Perception: 1 2 3 4 5 6 7 8 9 10 Satisfaction: 1 2 3 4 5 6 7 8 9 10
	Sense of Humor	Perception: 1 2 3 4 5 6 7 8 9 10 Satisfaction: 1 2 3 4 5 6 7 8 9 10
	Emotional Awareness & Coping	Perception: 1 2 3 4 5 6 7 8 9 10 Satisfaction: 1 2 3 4 5 6 7 8 9 10
	Work	Perception: 1 2 3 4 5 6 7 8 9 10 Satisfaction: 1 2 3 4 5 6 7 8 9 10
	Strengths	*What strengths appear to assist or to hinder your satisfaction in each component of your Creative Self?*

	Bridging Questions	"As you reflect on your areas of personal wellness, which do you believe might have been partly responsible for the concerns you entered counseling with?" "Which wellness areas might have assisted in keeping things from getting worse and your head above water?"
	Future Questions	"Often as counseling goals are reached, areas of wellness also shift. Which wellness areas will be different as life becomes more on track? How will they look different then in comparison to now?" "Imagine yourself in the future when you feel more in balance with your overall wellness. Tell me where you are, what you are doing and saying, and what others around you are doing and saying."
	Strength Questions	"What do you know or are learning about you that will contribute to successfully meeting your counseling and wellness goals?" "What other strengths will you need to tap into to overcome the challenges ahead as you begin the work of change?"

Resilience for the Strength-Centered Counselor

Adversity has the effect of eliciting talents, which in prosperous circumstances would have lain dormant.

–Horace

CHAPTER 11

Becoming a Competent Strength-Centered Counselor

We are privy to secrets that the clients are barely willing to share with themselves. We know the clients at their best and at their worst. And as a function of spending so many intense hours together, our clients come to know us as well. We are partners in a journey.

–Jeffery Kottler

In this final section, we hope to provide clarity not only of the development process associated with integrating a strength-centered counseling approach, but also of the tools necessary for you to manage "moments of frustration and bewilderment" when gaining a "greater conception of yourself." When learning a postmodern approach like strength-centered counseling, practitioners are confronted with a paradox stemming from their training in traditional and prescribed models of counseling. As Schon (1987) eloquently summarized, "in order to gain that sense of competence, control, and confidence that characterize professionals, students of professional practice must first give it up" (p. 72). Strength-centered counseling asks you to brave the discomfort of the unknown and to apply principles and skills that can often feel counterintuitive to your counselor training. It requires a willingness to view others, not from a perspective of deficits, but from a perspective that recognizes life struggles as patterns of personal resilience often unrecognized by the clients themselves or others. Strength-centered counselors approach each counseling encounter with an unwavering trust in the self-healing properties of individuals and purposefully utilize a language of strengths and possibilities. Most important, you will discover that your clients arrive at the first counseling session in possession of strengths and resources that will be the basis for supporting lasting change in their lives.

Applying this new perspective to your practice as a counseling professional can awaken anxieties related to integrating these conceptual shifts in your professional development as a strength-centered counselor.

I need a growth spurt. Adolescents can grow a couple of inches and gain a dozen pounds over the course of a summer. Boys' voices can squeak one day and drop four octaves the next. As a counselor, and moreover as a strength-centered counselor, I am lingering in prepubescence. The concepts are fresh in my mind and my practicum clients are there for the counseling, but somewhere in the midst of that, I am still too "young" to be effective.

To translate all the facts, theories, skills, and prowess of strength-centered counseling into my own practice leaves me feeling like a 90 pound, 13-year-old boy still in falsetto. Maybe expecting it to happen overnight is unrealistic . . . even waiting a whole summer is unrealistic. But as I continue to laboriously practice these skills . . . I pray for a growth spurt.

As a strength-centered counselor, I suppose you would ask, "What does a growth spurt look like to you?" Seriously, what it looks like to me, in me, is that I can sit before a client and have these little nuggets of wisdom and techniques in a queue in my brain ready to be offered at just the right time. That instead of feeling so anxious and nervous about getting it all "out there" before I forget, I would remain calm and these items would topple naturally from my brain to my mouth. To answer the "what could you do to get there" question, I would answer practice, read and reread notes and literature, and meet up with other students from our strength-centered counseling class. –Melissa R.

THEMES OF COUNSELOR DEVELOPMENT

The journey of becoming a competent strength-centered counselor will be as unique and varied as each of you, so understanding several themes of development might assist with navigating the bumps and challenges along the way. Professional development is a slow, long-term, continuous process that began even before your formal training as a counselor (e.g., through helping roles within your community) and lasts throughout your career (Rønnestad & Skovholt (2003). Adapted from the work of Rønnestad and Skovholt, we have included seven themes of development for strength-centered counselors. Each of these themes highlights a part of the necessary changes you will experience. The themes of counselor development along with the associated qualities exhibited by strength-centered counselors are set out in Table 11.1.

Table 11.1   Themes of Counselor Development

Themes of Counselor Development	Qualities of Strength-Centered Development
1. Integration	Strength-centered counselors gain an increased level of comfort in perceiving both personal and professional relationships from a strength-centered perspective where one influences the other.
2. Emergence	Strength-centered counselors experience a cognitive shift from performing strength-centered skills toward focusing on the worldview and experiences of others within which strength-centered skills naturally emerge.
3. Reflectivity	Strength-centered counselors maintain a commitment to learning strength-centered counseling embodied within continuous reflection on how the perspectives and skills are applied with clients and families.

Themes of Counselor Development	Qualities of Strength-Centered Development
4. Acceptance	Strength-centered counselor professional development is accepted as a slow and continuous process that can also be experienced as sudden bursts of growth, insight, and inspiration.
5. Tolerance	Strength-centered counselors experience increased confidence in managing the tension associated with balancing multiple professional perspectives (e.g., modern and postmodern) with the inherent ambiguity of the counseling process and human change.
6. Heroism	Strength-centered counselors realign themselves as benevolent helpers to a perspective where clients can heal themselves and are the "primary teachers" of their own lives, seeing the client as "Hero."
7. Inspiration	Strength-centered counselors demonstrate a willingness to seek inspiration from others in developing as a strength-centered counselor as well as becoming inspiring to others.

Over the course of continued training in strength-centered counseling, working with clients and colleagues from this perspective and recognizing the signs of your own growth as a counselor (e.g., realizing the influence of integration, emergence, reflectivity, acceptance, tolerance, heroism, and inspiration), you will gain competence.

STRENGTH-CENTERED COMPETENCE CONTINUUM

Strength-centered competence can be measured along a continuum with deficit-based destructiveness on one end and strength-centered proficiency on the other end. If you have been trained in traditional counseling practices, you may feel the tug of the familiar pulling at you to return to modernist training methods, practices, and paradigms as you move toward strength-centered proficiency. Students and counselors new to the perspective often feel that in order to embrace strength-centered counseling, they must let go of their previous training.

I will "George Costanza" my counseling practice, and hopefully everything I do. Oh do not fret, this is quite profound. On the sitcom *Seinfeld* the character George Costanza lives with his parents, is unemployed, socially awkward, and his robust physique is otherwise unattractive to women by typical societal standards. So the character perpetually lies in order to obtain the first date. Within a very short amount of time, each relationship ends in disaster for the character. During one particular episode, George finally realizes that that honesty might be the best policy; therefore, he decides he is going to "do everything opposite." He chooses to be entirely honest with women, informing them of his entire situation, and because this is television and not real life, his tactic works. He finds himself dating several women who are surprisingly interested in him emotionally and physically.

So from here on, I plan to do everything opposite as counselor. In lieu of a medical model or modernistic approach, which has been the basis of my education, I will strive to become a Strength-Centered Counselor. I will "do everything opposite" of what I was taught, I will "George Costanza" my practice.

My eyes have been opened to another way of thinking not only about my clients/students but also about myself . . . [strength-centered counseling] gave me the most hands-on techniques which can be applied among the most diverse clients and settings. One of the things I realized is that not only is it important for me to have the ability to help a [client] identify his or her own character strengths but, in order to be an effective counselor I must understand my own and the dichotomies as well. –Laura M.

With good humor, Laura M. expresses the same sentiment as many new to the strength-centered perspective. Moving toward and achieving strength-centered proficiency feels like practicing counseling methods in opposition to how so many of us were trained. To understand better where you are along the competence continuum, consider Figure 11.1. Adapted from work by Elsie Smith (2006) in strength-based counseling, this competence continuum can be used as a conceptual map of developmental levels related to your growth as a strength-centered counselor.

Figure 11.1   Strength-Centered Competence Continuum

	1st Level	2nd Level	3rd Level
	Deficit Based	**Precompetence**	**Strength-Centered Competence**
	Focuses on diagnostic labeling for treatment planning	Realizes that clients respond to more positive interventions, but has only a vague notion of Strength-Centered Counseling	Focuses on solutions and empathically appreciates the world view and life experiences of the client

Deficit-Based Destructiveness

Strength-Centered Proficiency

Source: Adapted from Smith (2006).

First Level: Deficit-Based Destructiveness

Following instruction within a traditional counseling education program, counselors may find themselves at the first level of the Strength-Centered Competence Continuum. At the first level, counselors work from a deficit-focused paradigm, placing themselves in the position of authority over clients. Formal introduction to a deficit-based model of counseling starts during graduate studies. Counselor education programs across the country require that students not only be familiar with the language of traditional clinical psychology but also be well versed in terminology and diagnoses presented in the *Diagnostic and Statistical Manual of Mental Disorders IV-TR* (*DSM-IV-TR;* American Psychiatric Association [APA], 2000). After graduation, new counselors join agencies and practices that also require proficiency in diagnostic terminology. Counselors act as experts who depend on the use of diagnostic labeling for treatment planning and sorting clients into diagnostic categories. Within counseling centers, practices, and agencies, counselors interact with clients and colleagues, using the language of traditional clinical psychology, focusing on what is going wrong in a client's life. Clients leaving such sessions find themselves feeling drained and possibly experiencing a lower sense of self-efficacy because of the session's almost exclusive focus on the negative, presenting problem (Saleebey, 2001). These counselors may lack hope-instilling skills and may not be aware of the client's strengths and resiliency in coping.

In our present education and mental health services delivery systems, it is as though counselors are encouraged to operate at the first level. Counselors communicate with other mental health and social support professions using language that labels the client as his or her presenting problem, expecting that all communication, written and verbal, use diagnostic terminology, working toward group identification and general assumptions, rather than individual possibilities and specifics. Once a counselor assesses a client, for example as "a depressive," the client relies on the counselor's expertise, and the counselor relies on written standards for assessment and treatment resources, such as the *DSM-IV-TR* (APA, 2000) and the Practice Planner Series (Jongsma, Petterson, & McInnis, 2006).

> Working with my first client during graduate training is where I met the all-powerful diagnosis. The client was agitated upon arrival to the session, and for me, as a student counselor, it was unnerving. The client had an energy that was unfamiliar; people during day-to-day interactions just didn't act like she was acting. Without much more than the preceding description, my supervisor said, "she's borderline." My first reaction was, "How do you know from a 30-second description?" The client was forgotten, and in front of us in our discussion was the "borderline." I felt sucked into the diagnosis. What if the client is something more than the symptoms that showed up that day? –Lynn P.

Second Level: Precompetence

Counselors who have noticed that clients respond well to more positive interventions but have only a vague notion of strength-centered counseling may find themselves at the second level of the continuum: precompetence. These counselors struggle with better meeting the needs of clients when their own training and supervision are largely problem centered. They have an increased sense that traditional approaches have limitations, especially with youth and minorities. Counselors at the second level may have had some training in strength-centered counseling, but they may not have had the benefit of supervised practice or much experience working with clients from a strength-centered perspective. These counselors have begun to form a commitment to practicing strength-centered counseling, trying out strength-centered language with clients and colleagues. One danger faced by precompetent strength-centered counselors is that when in unfamiliar and/or difficult situations, they may resort back to familiar counseling frameworks based on deficit-based understandings, organizational ideologies, and techniques.

Counselors at the second level find themselves in that nebulous professional space between understanding the notion and skills of strength-centered counseling and actually putting them to practice—professionally and personally. As Melissa R. mentions above in her description of needing a growth spurt, practice and reasonable professional risk taking can make a difference. This is the essence of increasing our clinical confidence with others and embodies a willingness to reflect on our own growing strength-centered practice, to seek supervision and additional training opportunities, and to maintain openness to the ups and downs of professional growth. This experience is true in relation to the change that clients and families seek for themselves, and it is true for you.

> I have trouble with the timing of when to use which tool, presenting it in the right language, gauging when to shift gears, ensuring a nice flow while staying present. Again, I am a Pee Wee ballplayer in a Major League Game. At least that's how I feel. Though like a ballplayer, I know it takes practice, practice, practice; but I need to practice with a coach or team. This is where an SCC group, if assembled, would really be beneficial. . . . It really is in the application, the practice, that these skill sets will finally click and feel more natural and the growth spurt will be achieved.
> –Melissa R.

Third Level: Competence

Competent strength-centered counselors work with clients at the third level of the continuum. These counselors have gained training in the principles of strength-centered counseling: They understand that trauma, abuse, illness, and life's struggles can be not only injurious but also the source of challenges and opportunities. Competent strength-centered counselors focus on solutions and empathically appreciate the worldview and the life experiences of clients, having mastered the use of a strength-centered vocabulary. In addition, competent strength-centered counselors have accumulated experience in working with clients from a strength-centered perspective, so that the idiosyncrasies of individual sessions can be handled without reverting back to deficit-based practices. These counselors are both able to adhere to the essential principles of strength-centered counseling and maintain the necessary shift in language for creating environments that support long-term change for their clients. Beyond client sessions, competent strength-centered counselors resist working with mental health professionals who come from a deficit perspective, instead focusing on client strengths, resources, and resilience. Finally, competent strength-centered counselors realize the positive influence of *strength centeredness* in their personal lives. Living out the essential principles of strength-centered counseling within a counselor's everyday interactions and relationships with family, friends, and colleagues creates a sturdy foundation for counselors to work as helping professionals.

With each interaction you experience the chance for growth. Your awareness, intentionality, and readiness will determine the influence of each interaction on your personal and professional development. Strength-centered counselors are aware that the journey from deficit-based destructiveness to strength-centered proficiency is a continuous process that will take intentional practice in integrating a strength-centered perspective in professional and personal interactions. Throughout this process strength-centered counselors experience continuous reflection on how the perspectives and skills are applied with clients, and they are able to manage the tension associated with balancing multiple professional perspectives (e.g., modern and postmodern) with the inherent ambiguity of the counseling process and human change. Strength-centered counselors relinquish control to the client as the expert on his or her life, realizing that clients have within themselves the strengths for self-healing and resilience. Readiness for growth as a strength-centered counselor is apparent through a willingness not only to seek inspiration from others but also to become an inspiration for others, and strength-centered competence emerges as the counselor makes a cognitive shift from a focus on performance of skills to authentic understanding and practice.

PROFESSIONAL GROWTH ACTIVITY: ASSESSING READINESS FOR COMPETENCE

For this activity, consider Figure 11.1. Strength-Centered Competence Continuum.

- Where do you find yourself on the continuum?
- Where would you like to be on the continuum?

To better understand your relationship to your own professional development, consider the Readiness Ruler (first presented in Chapter 7):

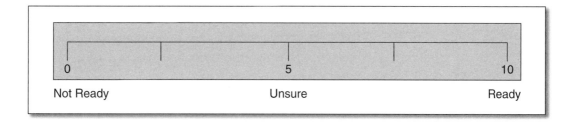

Working with a learning partner, or in your journal, answer the following questions:

- On a scale from 0 to 10, with 0 indicating that you are not ready to make a change and 10 indicating that you are completely ready, where would you place yourself on the Readiness Ruler for making necessary changes in your strength-centered counselor competence?
- How would you like to be able to rate your readiness for pursuing a shift toward greater strength-centered competence?
- What would indicate to you that you are moving toward greater competence as a strength-centered counselor?

CHAPTER 12

A Strength-Centered Counselor's Survival Guide

The journey of a thousand miles begins beneath one's feet.

–Lao Tzu

In Chapter 1 we introduced the nine essential principles of strength-centered counseling—a set of shared ideologies. As you approach the end of this text, we hope that you have come to understand the full meaning of the *shared* nature of these essential principles. Snyder (1994) suggested that individuals find hope when they discover pathways that lead them to their goals, and doing this within the shared bonds of interpersonal relationships leads to greater success. Reaching counseling goals and working with clients to realize their preferred lives is the most basic aspect of the shared nature of strength-centered counseling. The daily demands of working as a counselor (e.g., seeing clients, scheduling, attending meetings, continuing education) may allow little meditative time between appointments, but as you prepare to engage in this intimate and rigorous activity, it is helpful to find moments of quiet to recommit yourself to your stance as a strength-centered counselor.

In much the same way as Carl Rogers (1977) reflected on his presence prior to meeting with clients, the following is a reflective guide to assist you in maintaining focused intentionality on the nine essential principles of strength-centered counseling when preparing to interact with others.

FOCUSED INTENTIONALITY: THE NINE ESSENTIAL PRINCIPLES

Principle 1: A Shared Understanding

Reflective Question: Will I be able to share with others the unique qualities and strengths demonstrated in their efforts to stand up to life's difficulties while promoting a hope for change?

Reflective Statement: I will approach clients from a stance of acceptance, empathic curiosity, and an appreciation for the ambivalence inherent in their struggles for better lives. I will seek to appreciate the strengths that clients discover in our time together while trusting their potential for change and self-healing.

Most explicitly, you will strive to establish a *shared understanding* with clients during Phase 1 of strength-centered counseling, adopting a stance of empathic curiosity, acceptance, and appreciation for ambivalence in order to work with clients and colleagues to find a mutually understood perception of your clients' struggles and the strengths present within those struggles. Finding this common ground will assist you in guiding your clients to discover the strengths and resources already present within themselves, and to see how these strengths in some ways may be causing roadblocks on the path to change.

Establishing a *shared understanding* with your clients, as well as with your colleagues, is indicative of the curiosity you will rely on to discover how struggles impact clients' lives and how individuals are able to stand up to adversity, even thriving in some areas. Rather than mainly depending on symptom constellations leading to diagnoses, a *shared understanding* between you and your clients allows you not only to see what is possible for a client but also to see what allows a client to experience the stories of his or her history differently, making way for lasting change.

Though the development of a *shared understanding* begins at the first interaction, this understanding must be continually checked and revised. Throughout the counseling process, you, your clients, and your relationships react and adjust to the change process, necessitating regular reconsideration: Do you and the client continue to share an understanding of the client's perspective? In addition, as counseling continues, new aspects of clients are made known, and these new strengths and struggles must be incorporated into your understanding because a client's worldviews continues to develop and be disclosed. This continuing process highlights the recursive nature of strength-centered counseling.

Principle 2: Shared Respect

Reflective Question: Will I be able to respect the culture, gender, race, age, profession, financial and legal status, sexual orientation, religion, education, and various other roles people bring to their lives that influence an individual's life perspectives and personal understanding?

Reflective Statement: I will respect the culture, gender, race, age, profession, financial and legal status, sexual orientation, religion, education, and any other roles that influence my clients' life perspectives and personal understanding. I will work to collaborate with my clients in order to discover those strengths, resources, and perspectives clients use in seeking their life preferences, respecting clients as having the last word on what they need to improve their lives. I will accept the worldview of my clients, appreciate what they want different, and remain curious about how language can introduce hope, possibilities, and a readiness for change.

Inherently present in every phase of strength-centered counseling is respect for the client as the expert on her or his own life. Much of this *expertise* has been shaped through the client's interactions with others, through racial identity, cultural traditions, generational cohort, sexual orientation, political ideology, and religious practices, to name a few influences. Your clients are the confluence of these group associations, rather than representatives of singular group identities. At its core, strength-centered counseling is multicultural, and you must consider cultural influences and engage a sense of respect for the intertwined nature of multiple cultural identities, which are unique for each client. Collaboration is enhanced by a *shared respect* between you, as you appreciate your clients' multicultural influences, and your clients, as they try to realize their life preferences. The shared nature of respect reaches beyond recognizing cultural identity to a respect for the *individualness* of your clients within their life settings, respecting not only diversity's influence but also the individual as being diverse within his or her groups. Strength-centered counselors accept and respect the worldviews of clients, realizing what they wish different. That these realities exist simultaneously precludes that there is only one way of being in the world (Hansen, 2010). Clients may find themselves playing out roles in their lives influenced at some points by their ethnic identity, at other times by their religious practices, for example.

In addition, within each of these cultural identities reside strengths that clients draw from their environments (Sue & Sue, 2008). You will encourage your clients through collaborative discovery of those strengths and resources in seeking "something different" through respect for their ways of being in the world. You may also work with clients to recognize the source and development path of their strengths. Exploring the cultural history of a client's strengths reveals more than the names of a few individual strengths (e.g., tenacity, loyalty, creativity); it also offers the client multiple examples of how those strengths have been brought to bear in the client's past, within the client's interactions.

Is it possible to experience empathy with another? If not, counselors would be able to serve only clients whose lives mimic their own. Developing a *shared respect* within counseling relationships answers the question of whether counselors can be effective if they are lacking personal struggles, histories, or cultural identities similar to those of their clients. Sue and Sue (2008) suggested that culturally competent counselors begin with respect for a client's ethnicity and background and should continue with explicit recognition and open dialog about differences between counselors and clients. As put forth by Smith (2006) in her model of strength-based counseling, culture is a major influence on the formation of strengths and how people perceive strengths in themselves and others. Understanding the role of a client's culture on the development of his or her strengths goes hand in hand with using these strengths to help you reinforce your client's faith in moving forward and realizing lasting change.

Principle 3: Shared Strengths

Reflective Question: Will I not only be able to recognize strengths in but also elicit strengths from my clients? Will I be able to speak the language of strength-centered counseling so that I will be able to cocreate strength-centered action plans with my clients? Will I be able to use strength-centered language so that I can support my clients in finding hope for living their optimal lives?

Reflective Statement: I will assist my clients in understanding their struggles through a context of strengths and possibilities rather than personal deficits and problems. I will elicit strengths that are often hidden by misery and protective strategies. I will help my clients use their strengths for developing the self-healing tendencies necessary for change.

By the time individuals either voluntarily seek counseling or are referred to counseling through their families, doctors, or the legal system, they often feel as though their lives are characterized by problems and failures. Through recognizing strengths within your clients' stories, focusing not on the factual accuracy of the telling but on the ways that clients deal with difficulties in order to have survived, you will help them realize the internal resources they possess.

You may be the first to *share strengths* with your clients, but through examining exceptions, searching for preferences, and building readiness in Phase 2 of strength-centered counseling, your clients will begin to accept the presence of strengths within themselves. Throughout all the phases of strength-centered counseling you will continue to explore the depth and possible breadth of specific strengths, as well as develop less-often utilized strengths, creating a greater set of resources for your clients for future resiliency. Continuing through Phases 2 and 3, *shared strengths* are central to effective goal setting because they ground a *preferred life* in familiar landmarks and contribute to the likelihood of successful therapeutic outcomes.

Principle 4: Shared Resilience

Reflective Question: Will I be able to elicit personal strengths from my clients in order to increase life resiliency needed to manage stress and cope with adversity? Will I assist my clients in developing action plans that will allow them to depend on their own resiliency long after counseling ends?

Reflective Statement: I will work to build client resilience through a process of strength awareness and application. I will understand how people are "stretched" by life struggles, which offers a glimpse of strength characteristics that support and distract in the search for personal freedom. I will collaborate with clients to restore their belief in themselves, helping them gain resilience for future adversity.

The main goal of a strength-centered counselor is to work with clients to a point that the counselor is no longer necessary. Ideally, a client is able to walk away from counseling with an understanding of his or her life preferences and the ability to utilize internal strengths and resources when faced with future struggles, demonstrating resilience in adjusting to new circumstances. You will help lay the foundation for resilience in Phase 1 while discovering a client's perspective and relationship to ambivalence and strengths. During Phase 2, resilience is explored further while recognizing life preferences and developing a readiness for change. You and your clients will create a shared understanding of their personal wellness and determine useful measures and routines for practicing personal preferences in Phase 3.

Additionally, through the use of strength-centered language during sessions, clients find the additional strength within themselves for describing preferences and appreciating their own strengths. As clients continue to face adversity and find new struggles throughout their lives, they must depend on the resilience gained in counseling to stay grounded when faced with heavy rain and strong gales. The discovery of strengths can lead to life patterns that increase resilience and well-being.

Principle 5: Shared Dichotomies

Reflective Question: Will I be able to assist my clients with understanding the dichotomies of their personal strength in hopes of broadening the array of strengths available to them for better addressing life's struggles?

Reflective Statement: I will help my clients understand the dichotomy of their own strengths, recognizing the dialectic nature of strengths and experience. I will open myself up to how my clients' strengths and patterns of resilience might, at times, hinder the hopes they have for themselves and others around them. I will work with my clients to understand that they need to draw on a range of strengths in order to stand up to adversity in their lives, both tapping into their most obvious strengths and working to develop their less-often recognized strengths.

The curious quality of strengths is that though they assist in efforts to overcome life challenges, they also can thwart those very same efforts. If you consider your top strength (discovered throughout this text or with the VIA survey from Chapter 6) you likely found awareness of how your strengths are beneficial, and how, if utilized exclusively, they are not. Strength-centered counseling not only assists with identifying client and family strengths but also assists with developing and broadening an array of available strengths for solving life's challenges. Strengthening something that may seem unrelated to decision making, such as a sense of humor, may provide a buffer that helps in making a decision about which you are unsure. Helping clients discover their strengths, and when best to use them, is as important as helping them see that particular strengths may be standing in their way.

Principle 6: Shared Language

Reflective Question: Will I be able to use language that encourages equitable relationships? Will I be able to shift language in order to cocreate, with my clients, a reality of opportunities and possibilities, rather than problems and limitations?

Reflective Statement: I will use strength-centered language to elicit meanings from my clients, to cocreate realities of possibility, and to help my clients view themselves as distinct from their presenting problems. I will maintain a shift in language that focuses on what is strong in individuals and what they can do and have already been doing in their lives to survive and to thrive.

Beginning in Phase 1, your work as a strength-centered counselor depends on shifting your language to possibilities and strengths in order to discover a shared understanding with clients. Strength-centered language is a tool for demonstrating your own curiosity about your client's perspective while engaging your client's curiosity in the change process. Asking how the impacts of their struggles have robbed them of important hopes is using language that shifts away from what is wrong and toward an appreciation and acceptance of the unique personal qualities of the people you serve.

In Phase 2, you discover that the way you use language not only creates opportunities for clients to perceive themselves and their life differently but influences the development of preferred life reality. The language of possibilities and adding something to a client's life, rather than merely removing symptoms, is ever present when using the Miracle, Dream, or Future questions.

The strategic use of language again plays a key role when introducing lifestyle choices and personal wellness in Phase 3. Many clients will be exposed to the idea of the *Indivisible Self* for the first time. The language used to describe the five core *selves* with the related strengths and practices, provides clients the opportunity to interface with these concepts. Strength-centered counseling deliberately uses language to create with others an environment that surrounds the counseling relationship while providing opportunities to create, together, possibilities, hope, choice, and renewal.

Principle 7: Shared Wellness

Reflective Question: Will I be able to identify my clients' resilient qualities needed to address both their initial concerns and to work with them on increasing their personal wellness?

Reflective Statement: I will focus not only on my clients' finding relief from their immediate burdens but also on strengthening themselves to stand up to future adversity. I will accept that practicing personal wellness benefits both my clients and myself, when I, as a counselor, practice personal wellness to better withstand the professional struggles and fatigue that can accompany a career devoted to helping others.

Strength-centered counseling relies on adding that *something else* to a client's life. As strengths are uncovered and life preferences realized, clients begin to form action plans that depend on resources that are known to them (e.g., strengths). This increases motivation for client change: a change in his or her initial concerns as well as change toward ongoing lifestyle patterns and well-being.

A *shared wellness* is also a commitment strength-centered counselors make to themselves on behalf of their clientele. A commitment to personal wellness is introduced in Phase 3. Your experiences with the challenges and difficulties associated with lifestyle adjustment can offer a backdrop for introducing and working with your clients in understanding the interdependent connections among the five core aspects of self in relation to wellness.

Principle 8: Shared Hope

Reflective Question: Will I keep faith in the unique and surprising resources of people as they confront seemingly insurmountable odds? Will I keep faith that recognizing strengths and possibilities provides hope and the greatest likelihood for realizing preferences in my clients' lives?

Reflective Statement: I will remember the often seemingly imperceptible movements of change that reflect strength in my clients and offer hope for their futures. I will collaborate with my clients on developing trusting therapeutic relationships, for hope results from finding the way to our goals, partially by sharing them with others.

Your own sense of *shared hope* will increase as you witness your clients beginning to understand their struggles through a context of strengths and possibilities, rather than personal deficits and problems. This shift in perspective instills your clients with hope that change is possible, even probable, although, at times, the need to change is balanced by the need to maintain the present circumstances, producing ambivalence. Working with your clients to understand the validity in choosing *not to change* is as much a part of the counseling process as change itself. Often, creating a readiness for change is the first step in a *shared hope* between counselors and clients.

Past experiences of hopeful moments can also act as templates for the future as well as exceptions to the problems that clients might experience. Eliciting these hope statements from others can assist with increasing a readiness for change and a sense of hope that change will occur. Snyder (2002) observed, "A rainbow is a prism that sends shards of multicolored light in various directions. It lifts our spirits and makes us think of what is possible. Hope is the same—a personal rainbow of the mind" (p. 269).

Principle 9: Shared Authenticity

Reflective Question: Will I be able to work from the perspective of strength-centered counseling with my clients, with my colleagues, and in my personal life?

Reflective Statement: I will foster equitable relationships in both my professional and my personal life. I will respect myself and others, realizing that differences in individual choices are equally valid. I will practice the use of strength-centered language in looking for possibilities, solutions, and challenges, rather than limitations, problems, and setbacks, because language influences the reality of those in my environment. I will make a professional commitment to clients through a personal commitment to my own wellness and self-care.

"It is a delicately balanced ability," wrote Katz (1963), "which the empathizer has of being able to plunge into the sea of experience of another person and yet be able to climb out on the shore and regain his [her] own sense of self" (p. 144). This paradoxical stance illuminates both the immersion and extraction of therapeutic empathy; being able to do both requires dedicated thought and action. The experience of working with clients is hope instilling and satisfying, while at the same time is draining and, at times, overwhelming. How will you be able to be there both for your clients and for yourself?

Practicing as a strength-centered counselor is connected to your willingness to live out the nine essential principles of strength-centered counseling. It brings authenticity to the counseling process shared between you and your clients. Within and beyond your counseling encounters you will find that developing equitable relationships, self-respect, and appreciation for your own and others' life choices, even when different from your own, depends on a willingness to see "the best" in others as well as yourself. A *shared authenticity* is a commitment to practicing a strength-centered life with personal wellness practices. Here we present a Plan for Personal Hope and Wellness, which begins with active participation in living out the nine essential principles of strength-centered counseling in your own life.

LIVING OUT THE ESSENTIAL PRINCIPLES OF STRENGTH-CENTERED COUNSELING

These nine core principles are the foundation of strength-centered counseling and support the interactions between clients and counselors, moving individuals and families from the possibility of overcoming adversity to realizing a preferred life. These essential principles are interdependent and practiced together: resilience is enhanced by hope; understanding is grounded in respect; strengths are discovered through language. As you gain experience working with clients from a strength-centered perspective, these principles will become more concrete and intertwined. Counseling students and counselor educators should come to appreciate the integrated nature of these core principles as the essence of adopting a strength-centered perspective for work with clients, collaboration with colleagues, and for interactions in personal life.

CREATING A PERSONAL PLAN FOR STRENGTH AND WELLNESS

As you begin the practice of strength-centered counseling, you may find yourself at the beginning of a counseling career, or you may be in a place of renewal, where you are adding to your already working practice. In either case, you are at a point of change, which is a wonderful place to take several moments to center yourself and make a plan to strengthen yourself for the new adventure ahead. We suggest that you do something as simple as creating a Personal Plan for Strength and Wellness—strengths of mind, body, and spirit. This is a list of ways for you to protect the time you need for developing your interpersonal strengths and incorporating wellness and self-care into your professional routine.

> As I started my internship, one of the first assignments was to create a goals and activities sheet. Following the example from our text, goals one through nine covered topics like "Make Effective Use of Supervision," "Keep Up-to-Date on Paperwork and Preparation for Clients," "Investigate and Evaluate Appropriate Referral Resources," and "Establish Relationship with Agency Psychiatrist." Numbers nine and ten drew special attention from my supervisor, noting she'd never seen these kinds of goals listed before. Following Dr. Ward's advice from my practicum class, I included two goals: "#9—Build Trust in Myself as an Intelligent, Well-trained Counselor," and "#10—Maintain a Wellness Plan for Internship Duration." At first, doubting myself, I asked if it was ok to include the goals; of course I could take them off (reminder to self: work toward achieving goal #9). My supervisor said only that it was unusual, and she wished me luck.

On my own, I might not have rechecked my goals, but as we were assigned to reevaluate our goals midway through my internship, I was able to revisit those two points, and I noted that I'd only taken care to write them into my goals and activities list. From that point, I followed my plan and through the rest of my internship, and later through other challenging life changes, I have continued to consider my wellness and strength goals to help me strengthen myself through dedicated time for self-reflection, self-care, and personal wellness. –Isabelle V.

A Personal Plan for Strength and Wellness may take any form that works for you. A straightforward way is to make a list and to revisit the list perhaps every few weeks or months (see Table 12.1). As you gain more experience, and as you practice wellness and self-care, you may find that revisiting your goals is necessary less often. However, even the most seasoned counselor will find the dedicated time for self-reflection and self-evaluation is valuable for maintaining a strength-centered stance. Remember, the plan is personally tailored to fit you. Consider the essential principles. Where might you be strengthened with additional attention? Consider your five core selves as part of the Indivisible Self. How are you caring for each aspect of you?

Table 12.1	Example of a Personal Plan of Strength and Wellness	

Build trust in myself as an intelligent, well-trained counselor
- Understand I do not have to "label" everything immediately
- Recognize that my life experiences help me understand different perspectives
- Remain open to others outside my experience

Maintain a wellness plan for the duration of the internship
- Sleep enough
- Exercise
- Listen to music
- Protect some family time
- Read fiction

FINDING HOPE IN A PROBLEM-CENTERED WORLD

In their study of well-being, Ryff and Singer (1998) concluded that happiness was neither the goal nor a life pursuit, but a "by-product" of a life well lived. They believed this type of life illustrated an experience of the following six ideals:

- Autonomy
- Personal growth
- Self acceptance

- Life purpose
- A sense of mastery over one's environment
- Positive relationship experienced with others

Counseling provides a context not only for addressing initial concerns and problems but also for providing opportunities to address experience with these six ideals within our lives. To understand and approach people from a strength-centered perspective allows for an exploration of personal change beyond strategies aimed at symptom removal. It is designed to enhance one's resilience through an awareness of strengths and unique personal qualities to better address the challenges and disappointments of life. It is intended to assist others with "hanging on to oneself" while also embracing the hope that resides in despair and appreciating the solutions inherent in life problems. The suggestions below are to assist you in your development and to encourage a perspective of hope in a clinical world of pathology:

One

The journey of change is far more important than the destination. It is the decision to cast away from shore, in the face of uncertain struggles, that embodies courage and not the final port of call. Like any adventure, it is unpredictable, terrifying, exciting, and filled with hope for new experiences and, for most, a better life.

Two

Have faith in the strength of others and the often imperceptible movements of change. The difficulty of the trail is far more about the climb than the climber. Therefore, pay attention to the strengths and resources people apply in their daily lives that often go unrecognized. These are the building blocks of personal resilience and motivation for better lives and fulfilled relationships.

Three

Remember that the final goal of strength-centered counseling is not so much about feeling better as feeling stronger. Learning to soothe oneself when facing pain embodies a life with purpose and courage and is experienced by client and counselor alike. So, refrain from false reassurance and displaced optimism. These have little to do with a strength-centered perspective.

Four

Be a model of courage and empathic tenacity. Risk taking is the only road to increased confidence and self-efficacy. An empathic shared understanding of the experiences of others allows opportunities for counselors to take clinical risks grounded in the needs and hopes of those they work with, rather than themselves. As counselors, we are in the business of intimate conversations. Being bold demonstrates the very thing clients and families ask of themselves and reflects the reason they reached out for your help. Stand courageously with the conflict associated with discovery, and your clients will do likewise.

Five

Finally, trust the process of change. Stand firm in the words of Winston Churchill, who summarily described the attitude of professional resilience: "Never, never, never give up." You find in others what you believe to be true in yourself. If you have faith in the unique and surprising resources of people as they confront often insurmountable odds to a better life, you will find such . . . together.

Throughout this book you have heard from counselors new to a strength-centered perspective—about their frustrations, exhilarations, and the unpredictable consequences in relation to their professional growth as well as their personal experiences and those of others. The shifting of perspective is a difficult and daunting task. It requires a willingness to balance opposing views in a single moment and the courage to embrace ambiguity inherent in the complexity of human change as personal perspectives are discovered, revised, and/or transformed. The essence of this book is not learning the skills or interventions of strength-centered counseling, remembering the names of all the phases and each intervention, but of adopting a stance of being—it is not about the person as counselor but depends more on the strength centeredness of the counselor as a person.

PROFESSIONAL GROWTH ACTIVITY: A STRENGTH-CENTERED PERSPECTIVE AND LIFE ROLES

This activity is designed to enhance how a strength-centered perspective influences both professional personal life roles. In small groups, do the following:

- Each member write down five roles he or she currently assumes in his or her life and place each on separate pieces of paper, giving no hint to the other group members which roles were identified.
- Each member should decide which role he or she would be most willing to give up and toss it into the center of the group. Allowing equal time and opportunity for discussion, members should discuss why they threw the role away without discussing the content of the roles still remaining. Continue the cycle until only one role is left, and discuss why this role remains.
- As a group, discuss your reactions to the group activity while reflecting on how a strength-centered perspective might influence the roles in your life. Something to keep in mind is the focused intentionality of shared authenticity, as discussed earlier in this chapter and listed below:
  - o Do the roles you play out in your life allow for a sense of shared authenticity?
  - o What role(s) might you like to discard permanently?
  - o In addition to the role you kept during this activity, which other roles might you like to add?
  - o How does managing the number and type of roles you play influence your ability to work as a strength-centered counselor?

Appendix A
Counselor Interview &
Reflection Guide

Shared Understanding: The Stance

Focus	Intervention
Shared Understanding An Attitude of Curiosity	Professional Reflection Questions for the Counselor
	What does the struggle imply about the values and hopes of the client?
	What client beliefs are being challenged or possibly compromised in the face of the struggle? What does it mean for the client to have this struggle?
	What are clients learning about themselves? How have they sustained themselves in facing the struggle?
	What personal strengths have they needed to tap into? (See Table 5.2, Strength Characteristics)
	What does the struggle imply about what they would prefer different in themselves or their lives? What strengths will likely need to be developed in order to see this occur, even just a little?
A Stance of Acceptance	Professional Reflection Questions for the Counselor
	Do the clients know that you know the essence of the experience reflected in the complaints, implied in the symptoms, and transparent in the expectations illustrated within their narrative?
	What are the emotions, values, and strengths implied in the struggle and the hopes transparent in the conflict?

(Continued)

(Continued)

Focus	Intervention
Ambivalence Appreciation	What does his or her struggle with others tell you about the client? Does he or she know that you know?
	Ambivalence (Explanation Models) Questions for the Client
	"What is your theory about why change has been difficult for you?"
	"How have you tried to solve this and why have those efforts proved unsuccessful up until now?"
	"So, the problem is _____, and what you want is _____."
	Ambivalence (Change Models) Questions for the Client
	"In what ways would it be good for you to (action)?"
	"If you did decide to change, how would you do it? What would be your reasons for doing something different?"
	"What are the good things about change and what are the not so good things?"

Appendix B
Counselor Interview &
Reflection Guide

Shared Understanding: The Steps[a]

Focus	Intervention
Step 1: Problem Perception	Problem Perception "So, how were you hoping I could help you?" "Can you think of a name to call this problem? What is it like (picture/metaphor)?" "Are there other problems that this teams up with? In what ways does it do this?" Problem Impact "What impact has the problem had you/others?" "How has the problem robbed you of what you want?" "How does the problem 'get the best of you'? What has it promised you?" "What do you think will happen if you do not make a change?" Problem Influence "What does the problem whisper in your ear?" "Would the problem want you in counseling? How did it try to keep you from coming?" "How much of your life does it control? Is this your preferred way of being or would you prefer something else?" "Who else might be an advocate for you in standing up to the influence of the problem?" Exploring Explanations "What is your theory about why change has been difficult for you?" "How have you tried to solve this, and why have those efforts proven unsuccessful until now?"

(Continued)

(Continued)

Focus	Intervention
	"So, the problem is _____ and what you want is _____." Identifying Expectations "When things are more on track, what will be different in you as well as in your life?" "How will you know when counseling is no longer necessary?" Eliciting a Change Conversation "In what ways would it be good for you to change or 'do something different'?" "If you did decide to change, how would you do it? What would be your reasons for doing something different?" "What are the good things about change and what are the not so good things?"
Step 2: Struggle Perception	Strengths Within the Struggle "With all that you are managing right now, it makes complete sense you are tired and depressed. Your fatigue is likely more about the load you are carrying than about you. In fact, I am a bit surprised that things haven't become worse. How have you *managed* to keep your head above water?" "You found the energy and time to see me today. How have you *managed* to keep your sanity and hope in the midst of these problems?" "Talk about those qualities you have *learned* about yourself that assist in sustaining yourself in the face of stress. What would *others* say about the qualities that you have that keep you going during these periods?" "What *advice* do you give to yourself that helps you keep your head above water and reminds you to keep moving forward?" "When was the last time you felt *hopeful* about your life and circumstances? What was going on in your life that made you feel hopeful?"
Step 3: Strength Perception	Eliciting General Strengths "What are the best things about you? What is your guess about how they were developed?" "What special characteristics or talents distinguish you from others?" "What do you wish others might discover about you?"

Focus	Intervention
	"When are your strengths most useful for you? When are they not? What is your theory about this?"
	Anchoring Strengths
	"How might some of these attitudes, beliefs, and strengths be adapted and applied to your current difficulties?"
	"What strengths do you believe you need to develop to better address the difficulties we have discussed?"
	"How have you managed to keep things from getting worse?"
	Additional Strength Questions
	"What do you do well?"
	"What do other people look to you for?"
	"What are your outstanding qualities?"
	"How and with whom do you build alliances?"
	"How have you been able to adapt to change?"
	"Tell me what you do when you are at your best."
Step 4: Dichotomy Perception	Dichotomy of Strengths
	Summary of strengths (see previous steps)
	"Discuss how, despite your best intentions, these qualities/strengths get the best of you at times. How is this true in your current struggles? What other strengths might you wish to tap into instead during these times?"
Step 5: Hope Perception	General Hope Sequence
	"Tell me about a time you felt *hopeful* about your life and circumstances. What was going on in your life that made you feel hopeful?"
	"At that time, what *parts of yourself* did you have faith in? How might this have contributed to feeling more hopeful?"
	"When you felt more hopeful, how did you *remind* yourself to keep moving forward during difficult times?"
	Hope Chest
	"Let's suppose you could create a hope chest that would permit all your problems to go away. You can make a request to take out of the hope chest three wishes. Although the three hopes will be granted, you must make changes to ensure their continuation."

(Continued)

(Continued)

Focus	Intervention
	"What three hopes would you take out of your hope chest?"
	"How would the granting of these hopes change your present situation?"
	"What would you have to do to keep your hopes alive?
	What strengths do you have as a person to sustain your three hopes?"
	Patterns of Resilience
	"This has been very difficult for you. How have you *managed* to keep things from getting worse?"
	"What is your guess about how you developed these?"
	"What qualities do you *possess* that you seem to be able to tap into in times of adversity? What would *others* say are the qualities that you have that keep you going?"
	"What aspects of your heritage sustain you in times of difficulty? Who in your life was your 'cultural coach,' and what does he or she whisper in your ear? How is this useful to you?"

Note: a. When limited by time, a recommended abbreviated sequence is (a) Problem Impact, (b) Strengths Within the Struggle, (c) Dichotomy of Strengths, and (d) Patterns of Resilience.

Appendix C
Counselor Interview & Reflection Guide

Contracted Change: A Preferred Life

Focus	Intervention
Solution Efforts	Exceptions
	"When would you say the problem had less influence on you? How do you explain this?"
	"What is different about you during those times when the problem doesn't occur or has less influence? What are you doing differently? What advice are you giving yourself? What is happening differently around you?"
	"What do you do so that you don't have this problem then? Where did you get the idea to do it differently at those times? Whose idea was it to do it that way?"
	"Do you think this (problem/struggle) should speak for you, or do you think it would be better for you to speak for yourself? How will others know that this decision is becoming clearer for you?"
	Unique Outcomes
	"What do you do to keep the problem at bay when you need to? How were you able to weaken the influence of the problem?"
	"When does the problem have less influence on you? What is your guess about why?"
	"Has there ever been a time when the problem might have occurred but didn't? How were you able to do that then? What was different about you at that time?"
	"Who is in your corner regarding your efforts to reduce the influence the problem has on you and those around you? What advice might they provide?"

(Continued)

(Continued)

Focus	Intervention
Miracle, Dream, and Future	**The Miracle** "Suppose that when you go to sleep tonight, a miracle occurs, and because you were sleeping, you didn't know it happened. The miracle solved the problem that brought you here. When you wake up in the morning, what clues will you see that lead you to discover that this miracle has taken place?" "What else would be different?" "What would you notice in the advice you give yourself?" "Who would be the first to notice that something had changed?" **The Dream** "Suppose that tonight while you are sleeping you have a dream. In this dream you discover the answers and resources you need to solve the problem that you are concerned about right now. When you wake up tomorrow, you may or may not remember your dream; however, you do notice that you are different. As you go about your day, how will you know that you discovered or developed skills and resources necessary to solve your problem?" "What else would be different?" "What will be the first small bit of evidence that you did this?" "Who will be the first to notice and what will they see different in you?"
The Road Ahead	**The Future** "Imagine yourself in the future when the problem is no longer a problem. Tell me where you are, what you are doing and saying, and what others around you are doing and saying." "What else would be different?" Video Talk "If I were to *watch* you during the time when a miracle was occurring, what behaviors would I see you doing differently?" "What *advice* would you be giving yourself (cognitions)?" "What *would* we see you feeling (emotion)?"
Building a Readiness	Mind Mapping "What is your theory about how you were able to do that as you think about the miracle/future? How do you account for these changes?"

Focus	Intervention
	"What advice will you be giving yourself when the changes you are talking about begin to occur, even just a bit?"
	"How will you be able to stay on track in spite of all the distractions?"
	Intention of Change
	"What will you notice in yourself and those around you as you get more comfortable with 'idea' of the changes we talked about today?"
	Strengths of Change
	"What is there about you, what strong points that we have discussed or that you know about yourself, that could help you succeed in making this change? Who else knows this and could help in this change?"
	Hypothetical Change
	"Suppose that you did succeed and are looking back at the change now. What most likely is it that worked? How did it happen?"
	"What obstacles were you able to overcome and how?"
	"Suppose that this one big obstacle weren't there. If that obstacle were removed, then how might you go about making the change?"
	"Clearly you are feeling very discouraged about this. Use your imagination. If you were to try again, what might be the best way to try?"

Appendix D
Counselor Interview & Reflection Guide

Contracted Change: Understanding Goals

Focus	Intervention
Scaling Action Steps	Scaling
	"On a scale of 1 to 10, with 10 meaning things are completely on track and 1 meaning not at all on track, where would you put yourself today?"
	"Where would you like to be on the scale . . . what would you settle for? From where you are today, what would be a very first step toward what you would settle for? How would recognize that this was occurring for you?"
	"When the number on the scale is improved by one point, what will be going in your life, even just a little bit, that is not going on now? What would be a small step indicating to you that you are moving in this direction?"
	"Of the steps you mentioned, which do you have confidence that you can accomplish between now and the next time we meet? If not right now, which would you be willing to think more about and pay attention to between now and the next time we meet?"
Follow-Up Sessions	Follow-Up Through Scaling
	"On a scale of 1 to 10, with 10 meaning things are completely on track and 1 meaning not at all on track, where would you put yourself today since the last time we met?"
	"What is your theory about this?"
	"Of those differences that appeared helpful for you, what is your guess about how you were able to do this?"
	"What have you learned about yourself that has contributed to these differences?"

(Continued)

(Continued)

Focus	Intervention
	Follow-Up Through Change Awareness
	"What occurred between the last time we met that you would wish to see continue? What do you believe might have been partly responsible for this?"
	"What personal strengths were you aware of this past week? How do you see these making a difference? What did you need to overcome for this to occur, even just a little bit?"
	"What is the next step for you?"
	"Is there anything else you would wish to explore in counseling that might be helpful for you?"

Appendix E
Counselor Interview & Reflection Guide

Developed Lifestyle: Understanding and Practicing Personal Wellness

Focus	Intervention
Introducing Wellness	Steps to Introducing Wellness *Step 1: Orientation* "I feel like I am getting a pretty good idea of what you wish to accomplish during our time together. Often, counseling goals can reflect decisions that not only address your initial concerns but also work to increase your overall well-being and life satisfaction, as well as preventing future illness. Would it be all right with you if we take time explore how the counseling goals we identified might also consider ongoing lifestyle decisions?" • "What does wellness *mean* to you as you think about your life now?" *Step 2: Presenting the Model* "The following wellness model represents a way to look at ourselves as an interplay among our essential, creative, coping, physical, and social life aspects." (Show model and briefly define each core component.) "Before we explore these areas more fully, it might be helpful to start with your initial impressions." • "What strikes you about the wellness model?" • "As you consider the main headings in the circles of wellness, what things come to mind?" • "What areas of wellness do you believe might assist with successfully addressing your expectations for counseling?"

(Continued)

(Continued)

Focus	Intervention		
Envisioning Wellness	*Overall Wellness*	On a scale of 1 to 10, identify the number that best reflects your overall wellness and your satisfaction.	
	Overall Wellness	1 2 3 4 5 6 7 8 9 10	
	Satisfaction	1 2 3 4 5 6 7 8 9 10	
	Essential Self (Transcendence)	On a scale of 1 to 10, identify the number that best reflects your overall spiritual wellness and your satisfaction with your spiritual wellness.	
	Perception Satisfaction	1 2 3 4 5 6 7 8 9 10 1 2 3 4 5 6 7 8 9 10	
	Strengths	"What strengths appear to *assist* or to *hinder* your satisfaction in this wellness area?"	
	Coping Self (Temperance)	On a scale of 1 to 10, identify the number that best reflects your overall wellness in responding to life's circumstances as well as your satisfaction.	
	Managing Stress	Perception: 1 2 3 4 5 6 7 8 9 10 Satisfaction: 1 2 3 4 5 6 7 8 9 10	
	Sense of Worth	Perception: 1 2 3 4 5 6 7 8 9 10 Satisfaction: 1 2 3 4 5 6 7 8 9 10	
	Realistic Beliefs	Perception: 1 2 3 4 5 6 7 8 9 10 Satisfaction: 1 2 3 4 5 6 7 8 9 10	
	Leisure	Perception: 1 2 3 4 5 6 7 8 9 10 Satisfaction: 1 2 3 4 5 6 7 8 9 10	
	Strengths	"What strengths appear to *assist* or to *hinder* your satisfaction in each component of your Coping Self?"	

Focus	Intervention	
	Social Self (Humanity and Love)	*On a scale of 1 to 10, identify the number that best reflects your overall wellness in your daily relationships as well as your satisfaction.*
	Friendships	Perception: 1 2 3 4 5 6 7 8 9 10 Satisfaction: 1 2 3 4 5 6 7 8 9 10
	Love	Perception: 1 2 3 4 5 6 7 8 9 10 Satisfaction: 1 2 3 4 5 6 7 8 9 10
	Strengths	"What strengths appear to *assist* or to *hinder* your satisfaction in each component of your Social Self?"
	Physical Self (Courage)	*On a scale of 1 to 10, identify the number that best reflects your overall physical wellness and overall satisfaction.*
	Exercise	Perception: 1 2 3 4 5 6 7 8 9 10 Satisfaction: 1 2 3 4 5 6 7 8 9 10
	Nutrition	Perception: 1 2 3 4 5 6 7 8 9 10 Satisfaction: 1 2 3 4 5 6 7 8 9 10
	Strengths	"What strengths appear to *assist* or to *hinder* your satisfaction in each component of your Physical Self?"

(Continued)

(Continued)

Focus	Intervention	
Integrating Wellness	*Creative Self (Wisdom and Knowledge)*	*On a scale of 1 to 10, identify the number that best reflects your overall wellness in your skills for daily living as well as your satisfaction.*
	Problem Solving and Creativity	Perception: 1 2 3 4 5 6 7 8 9 10 Satisfaction: 1 2 3 4 5 6 7 8 9 10
	Sense of Control	Perception: 1 2 3 4 5 6 7 8 9 10 Satisfaction: 1 2 3 4 5 6 7 8 9 10
	Sense of Humor	Perception: 1 2 3 4 5 6 7 8 9 10 Satisfaction: 1 2 3 4 5 6 7 8 9 10
	Emotional Awareness and Coping	Perception: 1 2 3 4 5 6 7 8 9 10 Satisfaction: 1 2 3 4 5 6 7 8 9 10
	Work	Perception: 1 2 3 4 5 6 7 8 9 10 Satisfaction: 1 2 3 4 5 6 7 8 9 10
	Strengths	"What strengths appear to *assist* or to *hinder* your satisfaction in each component of your Creative Self?"
	Bridging Questions	"As you reflect on your areas of personal wellness, which do you believe might have been partly responsible for the concerns you entered counseling with?" "Which wellness areas might have assisted in keeping things from getting worse and your head above water?"

Focus	Intervention	
	Future Questions	"Often as counseling goals are reached, areas of wellness also shift. Which wellness areas will be different as life becomes more on track? How will they look different then in comparison to now?"
		"Imagine yourself in the future when you feel more in balance with your overall wellness. Tell me where you are, what you are doing and saying, and what others around you are doing and saying."
	Strength Questions	"What do you know or are learning about you that will contribute to successfully meeting your counseling and wellness goals?"
		"What other strengths will you need to tap into to overcome the challenges ahead as you begin the work of change?"

Appendix F

Strength Cards

Please refer to the Web site, www.sagepub.com/wardreuter for guidance in using Strength Cards during sessions with clients and for instructions to reprint additional sets of Strength Cards.

Honest

I am honest when I . . .

Genuine

I am genuine when I . . .

Authentic

I am authentic when I . . .

Diligent

I am diligent when I . . .

Industrious

I am industrious when I . . .

Tenacious

I am tenacious when I . . .

Energetic

I am energetic when I . . .

Enthusiastic

I am enthusiastic when I . . .

**Ability to exercise your will
even against opposition**

**Ability to exercise your will
even against opposition**

**Ability to exercise your will
even against opposition**

**Ability to exercise your will
even against opposition**

**Ability to exercise your will
even against opposition**

**Ability to exercise your will
even against opposition**

**Ability to exercise your will
even against opposition**

**Ability to exercise your will
even against opposition**

Lovable

I am lovable when I . . .

Caring

I am caring when I . . .

Generous

I am generous when I . . .

Kind

I am kind when I . . .

Intuitive

I am intuitive when I . . .

Playful

I am playful when I . . .

Good-Humored

I am good-humored when I . . .

Modest

I am modest when I . . .

Ability to appreciate those around you by tending to and nurturing relationships

Ability to appreciate those around you by tending to and nurturing relationships

Ability to appreciate those around you by tending to and nurturing relationships

Ability to appreciate those around you by tending to and nurturing relationships

Ability to appreciate those around you by tending to and nurturing relationships

Ability to appreciate those around you by tending to and nurturing relationships

Ability to appreciate those around you by tending to and nurturing relationships

Ability to appreciate those around you by tending to and nurturing relationships

Humble

I am humble when I . . .

Forgiving

I am able to forgive when I . . .

Cautious

I am cautious when I . . .

Merciful

I am merciful when I . . .

Discreet

I am discreet when I . . .

Prudent

I am prudent when I . . .

Self-Regulated

I am self-regulated when I . . .

Self-Controlled

I am self-controlled when I . . .

**Ability to demonstrate
consistency and moderation**

**Ability to demonstrate
consistency and moderation**

**Ability to demonstrate
consistency and moderation**

**Ability to demonstrate
consistency and moderation**

**Ability to demonstrate
consistency and moderation**

**Ability to demonstrate
consistency and moderation**

**Ability to demonstrate
consistency and moderation**

**Ability to demonstrate
consistency and moderation**

Astute/
Discerning

I am astute/discerning when I . . .

Curious

I am curious when I . . .

Open-Minded

I am open-minded when I . . .

Analytical

I am analytical when I . . .

Creative

I am creative when I . . .

Original

I am original when I . . .

Ingenious

I am ingenious when I . . .

Inquisitive

I am inquisitive when I . . .

**Ability to use your own
knowledge and experience**

**Ability to use your own
knowledge and experience**

**Ability to use your own
knowledge and experience**

**Ability to use your own
knowledge and experience**

**Ability to use your own
knowledge and experience**

**Ability to use your own
knowledge and experience**

**Ability to use your own
knowledge and experience**

**Ability to use your own
knowledge and experience**

Grateful

I am grateful when I . . .

Hopeful

I am hopeful when I . . .

Optimistic

I am optimistic when I . . .

Future-Minded

I am future-minded when I . . .

Spiritual

I am spiritual when I . . .

Believing in Faith

I believe in faith when I . . .

Appreciative of Excellence

I am appreciate excellence
when I . . .

Appreciative of Beauty

I am appreciate beauty
when I . . .

Ability to see a connection
between yourself and the larger
world around you

Ability to see a connection
between yourself and the larger
world around you

Ability to see a connection
between yourself and the larger
world around you

Ability to see a connection
between yourself and the larger
world around you

Ability to see a connection
between yourself and the larger
world around you

Ability to see a connection
between yourself and the larger
world around you

Ability to see a connection
between yourself and the larger
world around you

Ability to see a connection
between yourself and the larger
world around you

Even-Handed

I am even-handed when I . . .

Fair

I am fair when I . . .

Having Perspective

I have perspective when I . . .

Loyal

I am loyal when I . . .

Collaborative

I am able to collaborate when I . . .

Inspiring

I am inspiring when I . . .

Just

I am just when I . . .

Showing Leadership

I am able to show leadership when I . . .

**Ability to be fair and responsible
to yourself and others**

**Ability to be fair and responsible
to yourself and others**

**Ability to be fair and responsible
to yourself and others**

**Ability to be fair and responsible
to yourself and others**

**Ability to be fair and responsible
to yourself and others**

**Ability to be fair and responsible
to yourself and others**

**Ability to be fair and responsible
to yourself and others**

**Ability to be fair and responsible
to yourself and others**

Resolute

I am resolute when I . . .

Brave

I am brave when I . . .

**Ability to exercise your will
even against opposition**

**Ability to exercise your will
even against opposition**

References

American Heritage dictionary of the English language. (2006). Boston: Houghton Mifflin.

American Psychiatric Association. (1994). *Diagnostic and statistical manual of mental disorders* (4th ed.). Washington, DC: Author.

American Psychiatric Association. (2000). *Diagnostic and statistical manual of mental disorders* (Rev. 4th ed.). Washington, DC: Author.

Anderson, H., & Goolishian, H. (1991). Thinking about multi-agency work with substance abusers and their families: A language systems approach. *Journal of Strategic and Systemic Therapies, 10,* 20–35.

Ansbacher, H. L., & Ansbacher, R. R. (1967). *The individual psychology of Alfred Adler: A systematic presentation in selections from his writings.* New York: Harper.

Beedham, C. (2005). *Language and meaning: The structural creation of language.* Philadelphia: John Benjamins.

Benson, P. L., Galbraith, J., & Espeland, P. (1995). *What kids need to succeed:* Proven, *practical ways to raise good kids.* Minneapolis, MN: Free Spirit.

Berg, I. K., & Dolan, Y. (2001). *Tales of solutions: A collection of hope-inspiring stories.* New York: W. W. Norton.

Bertolino, B., & O'Hanlon, W. H. (2002). *Collaborative, competency-based counseling and therapy.* Boston: Allyn & Bacon.

Biswas-Diener, R. (2006). From the equator to the North Pole: A study of character strengths. *Journal of Happiness Studies, 7*(3), 293–310.

Bogar, C. B., & Hulse-Killacky, D. (2006). Resiliency determinants and resiliency process among female adult survivors of childhood sexual abuse. *Journal of Counseling Development, 84,* 318–327.

Boss, M. (1983). *Existential foundations of medicine and psychology* (2nd ed.). New York: Jason Aronson.

Bowen, M. (1978). *Family therapy in clinical practice.* Northvale, NJ: Jason Aronson.

Brown, S. D., & Lent, R. W. (1997). *Handbook of counseling psychology* (3rd ed.). New York: John Wiley.

Bryant, S. C. (2008). *Stories to tell to children.* Charleston, SC: Bibliobazaar.

Burns, D. D. (1989). *The feeling good handbook.* New York: William Morrow.

Cassell, J. (1978). Risk and benefit to subjects of fieldwork. *American Sociologist, 13*(3), 134–143.

Cepeda, L. M., & Davenport, D. S. (2006). Person-centered therapy and solution-focused brief therapy: An integration of present and future awareness. *Psychotherapy: Theory, Research, Practice, Training, 43*(1), 1–12.

Clark, M. (1997). Interviewing for solutions. *Corrections Today, 59*(3), 98–102.

Combs, A. W. (1954). Counseling as a learning process. *Journal of Clinical Psychology, 1,* 31–36.

Cormier, S., & Cormier, W. (1998). *Interviewing strategies for helpers: Fundamental skills and cognitive behavioral interventions.* Pacific Grove, CA: Brooks/Cole.

D'Andrea, M. (2000). Postmodernism, constructivism, and multiculturalism: Three forces reshaping and expanding our thoughts about counseling. *Journal of Mental Health Counseling, 22,* 1–16.

De Jong, P., & Berg, I. (1998). *Interviewing for solutions.* Pacific Grove, CA: Brooks/Cole.

De Jong, P., & Berg, I. (2002). *Interviewing for solutions* (2nd ed.). Pacific Grove, CA: Brooks/Cole.

De Jong, P., & Berg, I. (2007). *Interviewing for solutions* (3rd ed.). Pacific Grove, CA: Brooks/Cole.

Desetta, A., & Wolin, S. (2000). *The struggle to be strong: True stories by teens about overcoming tough times*. Minneapolis, MN: Free Spirit.

De Shazer, S. (1985). *Keys to solution in brief therapy*. New York: W. W. Norton.

De Shazer, S. (1988). *Clues: Investigating solutions to brief therapy*. New York: W. W. Norton.

De Shazer, S. (1991). *Putting differences to work*. New York: W. W. Norton.

Dimaggio, G., Salvatore, G., Azzara, C., & Catania, D. (2003). Rewriting self narratives: The therapeutic process. *Journal of Constructivist Psychology, 16*(2), 155–181.

Dolliver, R. H. (1967). An adaptation of the Tyler vocational card sort. *Personnel & Guidance Journal, 45*(9), 916–920.

Duckworth, A. L., Steen, T. A., & Seligman, M. E. P. (2005). Positive psychology in clinical practice. *Annual Review of Clinical Psychology, 1*, 629–651.

Emmons, R. A., & McCullough, M. E. (2003). Counting blessings versus burdens: Experimental studies of gratitude and subjective well-being. *Journal of Personality and Social Psychology, 84*, 377–389.

Erickson, M. H. (1954). Pseudo-orientation in time as a hypnotic procedure. *Journal of Clinical and Experimental Hypnosis, 2*, 261–283.

Flax, J. (1990). *Thinking fragments: Psychoanalysis, feminism, and postmodernism in the contemporary West*. Berkeley: University of California Press.

Fong, M. L. (1993). Teaching assessment and diagnosis within a DSM-III-R framework. *Counselor Education and Supervision, 32*(4), 276–286.

Frank, J. D. (1987). Psychotherapy, rhetoric, and hermeneutics: Implications for practice and research. *Psychotherapy, 24*, 293–302.

Frank, J. D., & Frank, J. B. (1993). *Persuasion and healing* (3rd ed.). Baltimore: Johns Hopkins University Press.

Frankl, V. E. (1963). *Man's search for meaning: An introduction to logotherapy*. New York: Washington Square Press.

Glasser, W. (1975). *Reality therapy: A new approach to psychiatry*. New York: Harper & Row.

Glasser, W. (1999). *Choice theory: A new psychology of personal freedom*. New York: HarperPerennial.

Gould, L. K., Ornish, D., Scherwitz, L., Brown, S., Edens, R. P., Hess, M. J., et al. (1995). Changes in myocardial perfusion abnormalities by positron emission tomography after long-term, intense risk factor modification. *Journal of the American Medical Association, 274*(11), 894–901.

Greenberg, J. S. (2006). *Comprehensive stress management* (9th ed.). Boston: McGraw-Hill.

Greene, G. J., Lee, M.-Y., Mentzer, R. A., Pinnell, S. R., & Niles, D. (1998). Miracles, dreams, and empowerment: A brief therapy practice note. *Families in Society, 79*(4), 392–399.

Gregory, R. L., & Heard, P. (2001). Border locking and the Café Wall illusion. Retrieved from http://www.richardgregory.org/papers/cafe_wall/cafe-wall.pdf (Reprinted from *Perception, 8*, 365–380 [1979])

Hansen, J. T. (2007). Counseling without truth: Toward a neopragmatic foundation for counseling practice. *Journal of Counseling & Development, 85*, 423–430.

Hansen, J. T. (2010). Consequences of the postmodernist vision: Diversity as the guiding value for the counseling profession. *Journal of Counseling & Development, 88*, 101–107.

Hattie, J. A., Myers, J. E., & Sweeney, T. J. (2004). A factor structure of wellness: Theory, assessment, analysis, and practice. *Journal of Counseling & Development, 82*, 354–364.

Heider, F. (1958). *The psychology of interpersonal relations*. New York: John Wiley.

Hoffman, L., Stewart, S., Warren, D., & Meek, L. (2009). Toward a sustainable myth of self: An existential response to the postmodern condition. *Journal of Humanistic Psychology, 49*(2), 135–173.

Jongsma, A. E., Peterson, L. M., & Bruce, T. J. (2006). *The complete adult psychotherapy treatment planner* (4th ed.). Hoboken, NJ: John Wiley.

Katz, R. L. (1963). *Empathy: Its nature and uses.* New York: Free Press of Glencoe.

Lambert, M. J. (1992). Psychotherapy outcome research: Implications for integrative and eclectic therapists. In J. C. Norcross & M. R. Goldfried (Eds.), *Handbook of psychotherapy integration* (pp. 94–129). New York: Basic Books.

Lent, R. W. (2004). Toward a unifying theoretical and practical perspective on well-being and psychosocial adjustment. *Journal of Counseling Psychology, 51,* 482–509.

Lent, R. W., & Lopez, F. G. (2002). Cognitive ties that bind: A tripartite view of efficacy beliefs in growth-producing relationships. *Journal of Social & Clinical Psychology, 21,* 256–286.

Lyubomirsky, S., Sheldon, K. M., & Schkade, D. (2005). Pursuing happiness: The architecture of sustainable change. *Review of General Psychology, 9*(2), 111–131.

Maddux, J. E. (2002). Stopping the "madness": Positive psychology and the deconstruction of the illness ideology and the DSM. In C. R. Snyder & S. J. Lopez (Eds.), *Handbook of positive psychology* (pp. 3–9). New York: Oxford University Press.

Maturana, H. R., & Varela, F. J. (1987). *The tree of knowledge: The biological roots of human understanding.* Boston: Shambhala.

Mezirow, J. (1994). Understanding transformation theory. *Adult Education Quarterly, 44*(4), 222–244.

Mikulas, W. L. (2002). *The integrative helper: Convergence of Eastern and Western traditions.* Pacific Grove, CA: Brooks/Cole.

Miller, G. (2001). Changing the subject: Self-construction in brief therapy. In J. F. Gubrium & J. A. Holstein (Eds.), *Institutional selves: Troubled identities in a postmodern world* (pp. 64–83). New York: Oxford University Press.

Miller, G., & de Shazer, S. (1998). Have you heard the latest rumor about . . .? Solution-focused therapy as a rumor. *Family Process, 37*(3), 363–377.

Miller, W. R., & Rollnick, S. (2002). *Motivational interviewing.* New York: Guilford.

Miller, W. R., & Rose, G. S. (2009). Toward a theory of motivational interviewing. *American Psychologist, 64*(6), 527–537.

Moyers, T. B., & Martin, T. (2006). Therapist influence on client language during motivational interviewing sessions: Support for a potential causal mechanism. *Journal of Substance Abuse Treatment, 30,* 245–251.

Moyers, T. B., Martin, T., Christopher, P. J., Houck, J. M., Tonigan, J. S., & Amrhein, P. C. (2007). Client language as a mediator of motivational interviewing efficacy: Where is the evidence? *Alcoholism: Clinical and Experimental Research, 31*(Suppl. 3), 40–47.

Myers, J. E., & Sweeney, T. J. (2004). The indivisible self: An evidence-based model of wellness. *Journal of Individual Psychology, 60*(3), 234–245.

Myers, J. E., & Sweeney, T. J. (Eds.). (2005). *Counseling for wellness.* Alexandria, VA: American Counseling Association.

Myers, J. E., & Sweeney, T. J. (2008). Wellness counseling: The evidence base for practice. *Journal of Counseling and Development, 86,* 482–493.

Myers, J. E., Sweeney, T. J., & Witmer, M. (2000). Counseling for wellness: A holistic model for treatment planning. *Journal of Counseling & Development, 78*(3), 251–266.

Nunnally, E. W., Miller, S., & Wackman, D. B. (1975). The Minnesota Couples Communication Program. *Small Group Behavior, 6*(1), 57–71.

O'Connell, B. (1998). *Solution-focused therapy.* Newbury Park, CA: Sage.

O'Hanlon, B. (2003). *A guide to inclusive therapy: 26 methods of respectful, resistance-dissolving therapy.* New York: W. W. Norton.

Ornish, D. (1990). *Dr. Dean Ornish's program for reversing heart disease.* New York: Ballantine.

Park, N., Peterson, C., & Seligman, M. E. P. (2006). Character strengths in fifty-four nations and the fifty US states. *Journal of Positive Psychology, 1,* 118–129.

Patterson, C. H. (1974). *Relationship counseling and psychotherapy.* New York: Harper & Row.

Peck, M. S. (1998). *Further along the road less traveled: The unending journey of spiritual growth*. New York: Touchstone.

Peterson, C., & Park, N. (2006). Character strengths in organizations. *Journal of Organizational Behavior, 27*(8), 1149–1154.

Peterson, C., Park, N., & Seligman, M. E. P. (2005). Orientations to happiness and life satisfaction: The full life versus the empty life. *Journal of Happiness Studies, 6*(1), 25–41.

Peterson, C., & Seligman, M. E. P. (2004). *Character strengths and virtues: A handbook and classification*. Washington, DC: American Psychological Association; New York: Oxford University Press.

Pilzer, P. Z. (2002). *The wellness revolution*. Hoboken, NJ: John Wiley.

Powell, J. W. (1987). *The exploration of the Colorado River and its canyons*. New York: Penguin. (Original work published 1875)

Prochaska, J. O. (2000). Change at differing stages. In C. R. Snyder & R. E. Ingram (Eds.), *Handbook of psychological change: Psychotherapy processes & practices for the 21st century* (pp. 109–127). New York: John Wiley.

Prochaska, J. O. (2007). High-impact paradigms for the treatment of addiction. In J. E. Henningfield, P. B. Santora, & K. Warren (Eds.), *Addiction treatment: Science and policy for the twenty-first century* (pp. 51–56). Baltimore: Johns Hopkins University Press.

Prochaska, J. O., DiClemente, C. C., & Norcross, J. C. (1992). In search of how people change: Applications to addictive behaviors. *American Psychologist, 47*(9), 1102–1114.

Prochaska, J. O., Norcross, J. C., & DiClemente, C. C. (2007). *Changing for good*. New York: HarperCollins.

Rak, C. F., & Patterson, L. E. (1996). Promoting resilience in at-risk children. *Journal of Counseling & Development, 74*(4), 368–373.

Rogers, C. R. (1957). The necessary and sufficient conditions of therapeutic personality change. *Journal of Consulting Psychology, 21*(2), 95–103.

Rogers, C. R. (1977). Characteristics of a helping relationship. In D. L. Avila, W. A. Combs, & W. W. Purkey (Eds.), *The helping relationship sourcebook* (2nd ed., pp. 3–18). Boston: Allyn & Bacon.

Rogers, C. R. (1980). *A way of being*. Boston: Houghton Mifflin.

Rønnestad, M. H., & Skovholt, T. M. (2003). The journey of the counselor and therapist: Research findings and perspectives on professional development. *Journal of Career Development, 30*, 5–44.

Russell, C. C., & Glass, J. S. (2002). Spirituality and counseling class: A teaching model. *Counseling and Values, 47*(1), 3–12.

Ryan, R. M., & Deci, E. L. (2000). Self-determination theory and the facilitation of intrinsic motivation, social development, and well-being. *American Psychologist, 55*, 68–78.

Ryff, C. D., & Singer, B. (1998). The contours of positive human health. *Psychological Inquiry, 9*(1), 1–28.

Saleebey, D. (1992). *The strengths perspective in social work practice*. New York: Longman.

Saleebey, D. (2001). *Human behavior and social environments: A biopsychosocial approach*. New York: Columbia University Press.

Saleebey, D. (2006). The strengths approach to practice. In D. Saleebey (Ed.), *The strengths perspective in social work practice* (pp. 77–92). Boston: Allyn & Bacon.

Santamaria, M. C. (1990). Couples therapy: Analysis of a "praxis" with a Freirian perspective. *Family Process, 29*(2), 119–129.

Seligman, L. (1996). *Diagnosis and treatment planning in counseling* (2nd ed.). New York: Plenum.

Seligman, M. E. P. (2002). Positive psychology, positive prevention, and positive therapy. In C. R. Snyder & S. J. Lopez (Eds.), *Handbook of positive psychology* (pp. 3–9). New York: Oxford University Press.

Seligman, M. E. P., & Csikszentmihalyi, M. (2000). Positive psychology: An introduction. *American Psychologist, 55*(1), 5–14.

Selzer, R. (1976). *Mortal lessons: Notes on the art of surgery*. New York: Simon & Schuster.

Shimai, S., Otake, K., Park, N., Peterson, C., & Seligman, M. E. P. (2006). Convergence of character strengths in American and Japanese young adults. *Journal of Happiness Studies, 7*(3), 311–322.

Smith, E. J. (2006). The strength-based counseling model. *Counseling Psychologist, 34*(1), 13–79.

Snyder, C. R. (1994). *The psychology of hope: You can get there from here.* New York: Simon & Schuster.

Snyder, C. R. (2002). Hope theory: Rainbows in the mind. *Psychological Inquiry, 13*(4), 249–275.

Snyder, C. R., Ilardi, S. S., Cheavens, J., Michael, S. T., Yamhure, L., & Sympson, S. (2000). The role of hope in cognitive-behavior therapies. *Cognitive Therapy and Research, 24*(6), 747–762.

Snyder, C. R., & Lopez, S. J. (Eds.). (2002). *Handbook of positive psychology.* New York: Oxford University Press.

Spence, D. (1982). *Narrative truth and historical truth: Meaning and interpretation in psychoanalysis.* New York: W. W. Norton.

Sperry, L., Lewis, J., Carlson, J., & Englar-Carlson, M. (2005). *Health promotion and health counseling: Effective counseling and psychotherapeutic strategies.* Boston: Allyn & Bacon.

Sue, D. M., & Sue, D. (1999). *Counseling the culturally different: Theory and practice* (3rd ed.). New York: John Wiley.

Sue, D. M., & Sue, D. (2008). *Foundations of counseling and psychotherapy: Evidence-based practices for a diverse society.* Hoboken, NJ: John Wiley.

Sweeney, T. J., & Myers, J. E. (2005). Optimizing human development: A new paradigm for helping. In A. Ivey, M. B. Ivey, J. E. Myers, & T. J. Sweeney (Eds.), *Developmental counseling and therapy: Promoting wellness over the lifespan.* New York: Houghton-Mifflin/Lahaska.

Sweeney, T. J., & Myers, J. E. (2009). *The indivisible self: An evidence-based model of wellness.* Greensboro, NC: Authors.

Tallman, K., & Bohart, A. C. (1999). The client as a common factor: Clients as self-healers. In M. A. Hubble, B. L. Duncan, & S. D. Miller (Eds.), *The heart and soul of change: What works in therapy* (pp. 91–131). Washington, DC: American Psychological Association.

Veninga, R. L., & Spradley, J. P. (1981). *The work stress connection: How to cope with job burnout.* New York: Ballantine.

Wagnild, G., & Young, H. M. (1990). Resilience among older women. *Journal of Nursing Scholarship, 22*(4), 252–255.

Wallis, C. (1996, June 24). Faith and healing. *Time,* pp. 58–64.

Walter, J. L., & Peller, J. E. (1996). Rethinking our assumptions: Assuming anew in a postmodern world. In S. D. Miller & M. Hubble (Eds.), *Handbook of solution-focused brief therapy* (pp. 9–26). San Francisco: Jossey-Bass.

Ward, C., & House, R. (1998). Counseling supervision: A reflective model. *Counselor Education and Supervision, 38*(1), 23–33.

Weick, A., & Chamberlain, R. (2002). Putting problems in their place: Further explorations in the strengths perspective. In D. Saleebey (Ed.), *The strengths perspective in social work practice* (3rd ed., pp. 95–105). Boston: Allyn & Bacon.

White, M., & Epston, D. (1990). *Narrative means to therapeutic ends.* New York: W. W. Norton.

Winslade, J. M., & Monk, G. (2006). *Narrative counseling in schools: Powerful and brief* (2nd ed.). Thousand Oaks, CA: Corwin Press.

Wise, M. (2001, June). *Expanding the limits of evidence-based medicine: A discourse analysis of cardiac rehabilitation clinical practice guidelines.* Paper presented at the annual meeting of the 42nd Adult Education Research Conference, Lansing, MI.

Index

Note: In page references, f indicates figures and t indicates tables.

About the Authors

Colin Ward's *Strength-Centered Counseling* reflects over two decades of clinical and academic experience. Frustrated by the limitations of traditional approaches to counseling for influencing enduring change with clients, Dr. Ward sought out additional training in postmodern approaches. He continued, in both school and private practice settings, discovering the phases of strength-centered counseling and then developing effective techniques and interventions for working with clients to engage hope, identify strengths, and develop resilient life patterns.

Dr. Ward is currently a counselor educator and supervisor at Central Michigan University. He received his B.S. in Education and Special Education from the University of Northern Colorado in 1983, his M.S. in Counseling from Winona State University in 1988, and his Ph.D. in Counseling from Oregon State University in 1997. In addition to strength-centered counseling, his interests include wellness counseling, school counselor training, advocacy and professional leadership, counseling supervision, family therapy, and public policy for promoting the counseling profession and social mental health.

Teri Reuter's wide range of professional and personal experiences have led her to believe in the transformational power of a strength-centered approach to counseling. Ms. Reuter has taught communication courses at the university level for over twenty years, and in that time, she and her family have lived in many different places in both the United States and Europe. Living in, working in, and adjusting to these varied cultures has helped her recognize the value of identifying one's own strengths and developing resiliency. In collaborating with Colin Ward, Ms. Reuter has refined her philosophies into practical guidelines to help her and other counselors work with clients in broadening their strengths and meet life challenges.

In 1989, Ms. Reuter graduated from the University of Florida with a B.A. in Communication Studies, and in 1991 she earned an M.A. in Communication Processes and Disorders and a Graduate Certificate in Gerontology. She received her M.A. in Counseling from Oakland University in 2008. Currently, Teri Reuter is in private practice in Orlando, FL.

Supporting researchers for more than 40 years

Research methods have always been at the core of SAGE's publishing program. Founder Sara Miller McCune published SAGE's first methods book, *Public Policy Evaluation*, in 1970. Soon after, she launched the *Quantitative Applications in the Social Sciences* series—affectionately known as the "little green books."

Always at the forefront of developing and supporting new approaches in methods, SAGE published early groundbreaking texts and journals in the fields of qualitative methods and evaluation.

Today, more than 40 years and two million little green books later, SAGE continues to push the boundaries with a growing list of more than 1,200 research methods books, journals, and reference works across the social, behavioral, and health sciences. Its imprints—Pine Forge Press, home of innovative textbooks in sociology, and Corwin, publisher of PreK–12 resources for teachers and administrators—broaden SAGE's range of offerings in methods. SAGE further extended its impact in 2008 when it acquired CQ Press and its best-selling and highly respected political science research methods list.

From qualitative, quantitative, and mixed methods to evaluation, SAGE is the essential resource for academics and practitioners looking for the latest methods by leading scholars.

For more information, visit **www.sagepub.com**.